WALK: A Memoir
My journey of faith and discovery after paralysis

Randy Krulish

WESTBOW
PRESS
A DIVISION OF THOMAS NELSON

Scripture taken from the Holy Bible, New International Version®. Copyright © 1973, 1978, 1984 Biblica. Used by permission of Zondervan. All rights reserved.

WestBow Press books may be ordered through booksellers or by contacting:

WestBow Press
A Division of Thomas Nelson
1663 Liberty Drive
Bloomington, IN 47403
www.westbowpress.com
1-(866) 928-1240

ISBN: 978-1-4497-5654-3 (sc)
ISBN: 978-1-4497-5653-6 (hc)
ISBN: 978-1-4497-5655-0 (e)

Library of Congress Control Number: 2012910862

Printed in the United States of America

WestBow Press rev. date: 06/26/2012

TO MOM

My loving Mother!

To the most extraordinary woman I know, my mother!
Mom, thanks for always being there and giving me support!
You never told me I couldn't do something. You always gave me
encouragement. How do I thank you for that? Just know you are my hero.
You are the best role model any son could ask for!
I will always love you!

THANKS TO JULIE

Julie Bigaouette

I would also like to give a special thanks to Julie Bigaouette!. Without her, this book would not have come into being. I never planned on writing a book. Soon it became apparent God used Julie to be the engineer to start this whole book writing journey.
Thank you, Julie!

CONTENTS

PREFACE

I was born December 18, 1953. Ever since I can remember, I was surrounded by my loving parents and caring siblings. For the first twelve years of my life, farm existence was all I knew. In my opinion, it's the best way to grow up. It's an unassuming lifestyle filled with simplicity. Those twelve years were magical—no worries, concerns, or stress.

My lifestyle changed forever on May 30, 1966. The magic was taken from me in a split second through a horrific accident that resulted in a broken neck. I will take you on a journey as seen through the eyes of a frightened twelve-year-old boy. I explain how God and family provided me with the necessary strength to endure my now unexpected life of paralysis.

Even though these newfound struggles were nearly more than I could cope with, I found the inner peace to overcome them. My true-life inspirational story will make you cry and laugh, but most important, it will give you hope! You will discover how my life was changed forever; it may change yours as well.

INTRODUCTION

Why would a paralyzed man choose the title *Walk* for his book? Whether it is physically, emotionally, or spiritually, we all walk through life. After my accident, I needed to learn to walk all over again. We walk on our journey, whether we can use our arms and legs or not. We don't just coast through life.

Someone once told me, "When a tragedy strikes you, your life will never be normal again, but you can start a new normal life." My life may not be normal in the sense that I'm paralyzed, but it's normal to me.

Sometimes the pain and suffering can seem to be more than we can handle, but it's during those times that we need God the most. We grow in our walk with Him during these times, and we learn to lean on Him for strength! As we grow in our Christian journey, we realize we need to turn to Him at all times, good and bad.

I want to share my story with others to simply offer hope. God has taken me on a long pilgrimage through life, filling me with hope as I go.

Walk with me on this wonderful journey God has blessed me with!

*I decided not to mention names of any hospital staff or other patients. There are likely many more people who did not get a specific mention, but they have not been forgotten. With the exception of family, all names have been changed to protect individual privacy.

ACKNOWLEDGMENTS

Thanks to Beth Erickson, of Jobe Communications, for the wonderful job she did editing my book. She spent countless hours pouring over it and had great suggestions. With her encouragement, I was able to dig deep inside myself and let the book reveal the feelings that had been locked inside for over forty years. When all the editing and suggestions were finished, I believe this book reflects the true me.

Westbow Press Publishing is a wonderful self-publishing company. They walked me through each phase of the publishing process. Westbow Press made sure my book was the best it could be. I would like to thank them for always being available and helping me to the finish line.

The reason this book was written is because of Julie Bigaouette. She suggested the book writing idea to me and I was not receptive. To my dismay, she continued to gently cheer me on. After much prayer, I realized God teamed us up to begin the book writing journey. Julie is the epitome of a true friend!

Dr. Lori Campbell M.D. was invaluable with self-publishing information. Dr. Campbell has self-published a book and helped get me in contact with my editor. I believe our connection was definitely God orchestrated.

Amanda Kauphusman helped with some early editing ideas and suggestions. This information was very helpful when writing the rest of my manuscript. Thanks Amanda, for your help and insight.

A big thank you to Sue Starrett for all the secretarial duties she performed. This included writing notes, addresses, phone numbers, picking up much needed supplies, and so much more. Thanks Sue, for always being willing to help!

Mary Peck, of marylandherrphotography.com, did an excellent job photographing the front and back covers of my book. Mary also scanned the pictures inside the book. Her knowledge of photography was extremely helpful. I appreciate her help so much. I never could've done this without her assistance.

I have a difficult time expressing my thanks for the financial donations I received to publish my book. The financial and prayer support was overwhelming. Please know I appreciate you believing in me from the start. Without you, this book would never be a reality. I truly believe a part of each and every one of you is in this book!

When it comes to my family, where do I start? God blessed me with an amazing family. You have always been there for me and given me constant support! Thanks for helping me reflect on the events during and after my accident. I promise to always be here for you. I love you and God Bless!

CHAPTER 1
AN IDEAL CHILDHOOD

*"Train up a child in the way he should go,
even when he is old he will not depart from it."*
—Proverbs 22:6

My fourth grade school picture (1964)

Growing up in a small farming community right on the Minnesota/Iowa border afforded me a lot of time for just living, exploring, and learning about life. Although so much would later change, in many ways, it was an idyllic childhood. I lived in a rural setting—simple, fun, yet not without small trials and tribulations that could easily be resolved.

Our farm was about five miles north of Lyle, Minnesota, and there wasn't a better place to grow up. My school friends from town were always trying to think of something to do to alleviate boredom. It wasn't that way for me. The farm was a peaceful and tranquil setting, but there was always work to be done or fun to be had. I loved the animals. We had cows, pigs, and sheep. When you're around them so often and caring for them, you develop a certain connection. We even named all the milk cows, such as Betty and Lucy. Because we fed them and cared for them, the animals were always happy to see us.

Though I had playtime, my siblings and I also had responsibilities from as early as I can remember. There was a twelve year span in the ages of my siblings. Jim was the oldest, and then it was me, Becky, Bob, and Linda.

GREETINGS FROM OUR HOUSE TO YOUR HOUSE

The Krulish's

**Left to right - Me, Bob, Jim, and Becky -
Christmas 1960, Linda not born yet**

No one was too young to help. We all had different responsibilities that were age appropriate. Since Jim and I were the oldest, we milked cows each morning, with Dad always right by us. I was often jealous of Jim because, as the oldest, he was always first to learn a new chore. He could operate a milker and some of the farm machinery before me. Eventually my turn came when Dad figured it was time. In addition to milking, we fed livestock, pitched manure, mowed the lawn, worked in the fields, and hunted with Dad. Jim was a good big brother. We were together most of the time, between doing chores and playing. We played catch a lot since we both played 4-H softball. Sometimes Dad played too. We thought it was pretty cool when Dad joined us. We also built with hay and straw bales in the hayloft for hours on end, built forts in our woods, and used the tire swing Dad hung for us. We were never bored.

Becky helped in the house, doing dishes and some of the cleaning. Of course, Jim and I never thought she worked as hard as we did. Becky—or Beck, as we always called her—had long, blonde hair. She was all girl. One day, a bat got into the house, and she feared it would get tangled in her locks. She grabbed a clothesbasket and put it over her head for protection. In the end, Dad got the bat out of the house. Since Beck and I were only eighteen months apart, we did a lot together. She was the opposite of me, very outgoing. I helped her learn to ride a bike and tie her shoes. During the school year, when it was time to walk down a long, dirt driveway to get on the bus, Mom told Jim and me to make sure we let Beck on the bus first. Jim didn't always listen, but I did for some reason.

The youngest two, Bob and Linda, fed our dog and did other simple chores to learn responsibility. Our neighbor used to call them Jody and Buffy, from the TV show *Family Affair*, because they had red hair and bore a resemblance to the characters. Bob was quiet, like me, and very curious. He was always investigating in our woods, once falling off of a fence and breaking his collarbone. He loved playing in the sandbox with his little plastic army men. And Linda? She was all tomboy and always wanted to be outside.

My parents were good, hardworking people. Dad grew up on a farm, and that's all he ever really wanted to do. He had a strong personality and was a great jokester and storyteller. He was a strong man with muscular arms. I wanted to be just like him. Every night, after milking the cows, we'd carry the milkers up to the house to be washed out in the basement. Dad could carry one with each arm—no problem. When I tried carrying them like Dad, I never seemed to hold them out from my sides like he could. They always fell against my legs and dangled as I walked.

Dad taught us to grease the machinery before we used it, respect the land, respect and use a gun properly, and so much more. We experienced the full range of farm life. We were even right there when the farm animals gave birth. Dad felt it was best if we understood all aspects of farm life. And watching a calf being born was nothing short of a miracle! Though he wasn't a big churchgoer, Dad still believed in God and felt closest to Him when he was out with nature and experiencing the cycle of life on the farm. I felt the same. Spiritually, I began connecting with God when I was a kid growing up on the farm. One of my favorite chores was working in the field. It didn't matter if I was spreading manure or rowing hay. I loved the smell of a freshly cut clover field! It felt liberating and even powerful driving the tractor. In the fields, I saw the endless blue sky, felt the gentle breeze in my face, heard the birds singing, and bore witness to life as the crops grew, wildlife romped, and flowers bloomed. Dad felt this was a time to think and thank God for all of our blessings. I did too.

As for Mom, she was the rock of our family. A very sweet lady with a strong spirit, she was the organizer who kept things running smoothly in our clan of seven. I always felt safe in her presence. She made our house feel like a home. Each spring, there was always a fresh bouquet of lilacs on the kitchen table. And I can still smell the homemade apple crisp that baked in the oven every fall. It was the little things that made all the difference. A couple times during the summer, we'd get to go to the drive-in theater, and Mom would always pop a big brown paper bag full of popcorn. We'd pass that around during the movie. We also got to dress in our pajamas because Mom knew we'd be asleep before we got home. At Christmas, Mom had us decorate cut-out sugar cookies and make faces out of the frosting. On Sundays, she made a fried chicken dinner that our whole family enjoyed. She made sure we always ate together at the kitchen table. We had real meat and potatoes meals. Some Sundays, we'd head to my grandparents or cousin's place, if Dad wasn't busy in the field. But we'd always come home early because chores needed to be done and cows milked. In any event, Mom made our meals very special. And she always had extra time for us. I remember lying on the grass with her and just gazing at the clouds. She could imagine the most amazing creations out of the clouds, which I couldn't see until she pointed them out. She used to talk about God's artistry being all around us. She was a person with a huge heart and soul. We went to church service and Sunday school fairly often, but probably wouldn't have been considered regular attendees. Even so, God's love shined through Mom. I felt His presence around her with all her kind words and actions. There's nothing like the love of a mother!

We never questioned or argued with our parents. What they said was the final word, and we accepted it as such. I can only remember one spanking from Dad. Jim and I were fighting, and Dad had had enough. We both had to bend over his knee and take the punishment we deserved. It was in no way a severe punishment. Dad simply disciplined us because he cared. He once told me, "If you don't lie, you have nothing to remember." It was some of his best advice. We learned that when you lied, it was hard to keep the lies straight. Telling the truth was always simplest. We respected our parents' authority. In fact, it hurt me to disappoint my parents, probably more than it hurt them.

Their discipline was a gift, but perhaps the biggest gift was their time. Whether it was getting in the car after dinner and searching for white-tailed deer, playing games, or watching television together, Mom and Dad took the time to be with us. They even made it fun when the electricity went out during winter storms, something that could last for two or three days. Mom would light these old oil lanterns. Dad kept the oil furnace going, and Mom gathered us around a lantern to do crafts.

We didn't have a lot of material things, but we had our parents' time. Though they were never affectionate toward one another in front of us, we knew they loved each other and us.

Mom and Dad's wedding photo (1947)

And, they were good neighbors—pitching in with no expectations when needed by others. They were both also part of the monthly card club. We loved when it was our turn to host. Mom would let us stay up long enough to help serve the food, which was a real treat.

Overall, I don't have a single regret about my childhood. It was a simple time—no hustle and bustle like today. At the farmhouse, we didn't have an indoor bathroom; we used an outhouse. We had a party telephone line, which means four or five farm families shared the same phone line. Each family had their own ring. One family's might be two short rings and a long ring; the next might be a short ring followed by two long ones. You never answered unless it was your ring. And if you wanted to use the phone, you had to make sure no one else was using it. If they were, you just waited until they were done.

We didn't have cell phones, computers, or other electronic gadgets to fill up our time. Instead, we turned to our imaginations. Many a summer night, we'd run about trying to catch fireflies. When we finally caught one of those wily bugs, we'd put it in a clear Mason jar and watch it light up. We also played games such as kick-the-can, tag, and hide-and-go-seek. We had our own version of baseball, hitting rocks with a piece of wood out in the pasture. There were a lot of homeruns. We did have a television, however. My parents loved westerns, so as a family, we watched a lot of them. *Gunsmoke* and *The Rifleman* were two of my favorites, but we also watched *The Andy Griffith Show* and *The Ed Sullivan Show*. Sometimes on Saturday mornings, we'd watch cartoons like *Popeye, The Roadrunner,* and *Tom and Jerry.* We only had three channels, but that was enough.

My childhood moved at a much slower pace than that of today's children. And we didn't have much stress or worry in our lives. Though we worked hard, we had plenty of time to stop and smell the roses. It was a childhood worth remembering; a childhood filled with rich memories, solid faith, and the love of my family; a childhood that could sustain me like manna in the desert no matter what path I would walk.

CHAPTER 2
THE ACCIDENT

"As a mother comforts her child,
so will I comfort you."
—Isaiah 66:13

I remember May 30, 1966, as if it were yesterday. Life changed for all of us that day. I was twelve-years-old that year, busy helping Dad on the farm and finishing up sixth grade. Jim was fifteen, Becky was ten, Bob was six, and Linda just turned three. And I couldn't wait for summer vacation to start. Summer meant Little League 4-H softball, and I loved sports and competition.

That particular day began as any other, with chores to be done. But, after, my four siblings and I were going swimming for the first time that year. The weather was warm, and we were anxious for a little taste of summer before school was even finished. After chores, we got in the car; met my aunt, uncle, and four cousins; and drove to a lakeside resort in Faribault, Minnesota. Dad couldn't come as he had to finish working some ground to plant beans. We were hungry when we arrived, so we ate a picnic lunch that my mom and aunt had prepared: fried chicken and potato salad.

We could hardly wait to go swimming. The water was crystal clear, and the surface looked like shiny glass. We chose to swim and dive from a dock on the water that we thought was a perfect place. It stretched for many yards into the water. We figured it was deep enough to dive in since Jim, who was much taller than me, stood at the end of the dock and the water went up to his chest and neck area. And it was plenty warm since it had been a warm spring that year.

My first dive was a belly-flop. Jim didn't laugh, but I figured he was giggling on the inside. His first dive was a good one. After witnessing that, and since I'm a perfectionist, I wanted to make my second dive memorable.

"Hey, watch this one!" I shouted.

Standing at the end of the dock, I looked down the length of it and pictured the dive in my head. Taking a deep breath, I slowly started running. Those were the last footsteps I'd ever take.

Even then, it was like slow motion. When I finally got to the end of the dock, I jumped as high as I could. It felt perfect! I turned downward, just as I had pictured in my mind, and shot straight down into the water. Everything was going as I'd envisioned. Although my hands weren't cupped above my head as they should've been, and they were too far apart, I still believed it had been a great dive. And although slicing through the surface of the water felt great, when I entered the water, everything changed. I went limp. My arms and legs wouldn't move. I had no pain at all. No feeling. Slowly, I floated up, face down.

I wondered what was going on. Did I have a cramp? I tried to take a breath and swallowed water. I realized I couldn't breathe and needed help. Panic began to set in. I had no idea what to do, nor could I move to help myself. Jim was my only hope. I knew he was watching, but where was he? Why was it taking him so long? It felt like I had been floating there forever. Finally, he turned me over. I tried to yell, but nothing came out. That breath of air felt so precious. Jim's face was filled with fear. He didn't say a word to me, and all I could do was look at him. He struggled to hold me. Since I was dead weight, I kept slipping through his arms. Again, the water engulfed me. I swallowed more water and thought I might drown. *Is this it?* I wondered. *Am I going to die?*

That's when I began to pray. *No! I don't want to die! God help me!* That's when Jim pulled me up again, and I took in another breath of precious air. He tried to lift me up onto the dock, but it was a losing battle. Thankfully, Mom, who'd been visiting with my aunt at a different beach area, was returning. As she walked back, she watched us closely. Something seemed wrong. Her motherly instincts kicked in as she ran to help Jim.

"Let's pull him to the beach area," she said.

I was never happier to hear her voice then at that moment. It was a miracle. When I saw her loving face, I knew everything would be okay. She had an intense look of concentration and clearly wanted to get me to safety. As my siblings, cousins, and aunt and uncle gathered around, at first, no one said anything. There was nothing but confusion. No one knew what had happened.

"What's wrong?" shouted my oldest cousin as she approached. No one answered because they didn't know. There were many questions, but no answers. I knew something was wrong, but everyone seemed frozen. Everyone wanted to help, but no one knew what to do. There was so much uncertainty.

Mom and Jim had moved me to the beach. The sun was blinding me as I lay there on the beach, unmoving. Jim held up a blanket to shield me from the sun. I could only speak the slightest of whispers. Looking back, Jim may have had a better sense of the severity of the situation than the others, because of what he had experienced firsthand trying to get me to safety. The look of fear on his face was unchanged. It made me nervous and confused me. It was hard for me to believe it was so serious because I felt no pain. I didn't cry because I didn't know what to feel. The only comfort was in having Mom at my side since she always made me feel safe.

Finally, someone from the resort shouted, "There's a doctor here!"

"Get him!" yelled my panicked Uncle Bob. A fireman, he arrived to help my mom with me, but couldn't. It was his greatest fear—to be needed at the site of an accident and be unable to help. This accident hit too close to home.

When the doctor arrived, he took a twig and touched my arms and legs with it.

"Can you feel me touch you?" he asked.

"No," I whispered, barely audible.

"How about now?"

"No," I said weakly. I didn't even know he had touched me with that twig in a different area, let alone that he was rubbing that twig up and down the bottom of my foot. I couldn't feel anything.

"Someone call an ambulance!" he yelled.

Fear began to set in again. *Why do we need an ambulance?* I wondered. Though people were shouting, I couldn't understand what they were saying. I couldn't turn my head to see what was going on, either. Mom was my angel of mercy. She kept touching me on my face. It felt so soothing. I knew only one thing for sure: Mom was by my side. "The ambulance will be here soon," she said reassuringly. Shortly after, I heard the sirens. When the ambulance arrived, they placed me on a cot. The doctor talked with them briefly. By now, a small crowd had gathered, and people were staring at me as the EMTs placed me in the ambulance. I didn't know what all the commotion was about. I only knew something was wrong. In the ambulance, they put a sandbag on each side of my head to keep it as immobile as possible. Mom rode along with me. I can't imagine taking that long, scary trip without her by my side. At one point, we even had to change ambulances before we headed to St. Marys Hospital in Rochester. The one I was in didn't have enough gas to reach our destination. The sirens were blaring, but the driver was very upset because other drivers wouldn't pull over to let us pass. "Pull over. We need to get through!" he'd yell. I didn't realize it then, but time was of the essence.

The other attendant kept reassuring us, saying, "We'll be in Rochester soon." I didn't understand the urgency. Mom didn't know what was wrong either. She prayed, desperately, all the way to Rochester, "God, please let Randy be okay."

CHAPTER 3
ST. MARYS HOSPITAL

"Hope does not disappointment us."
—Romans 5:5

When we got to the emergency room, there was a mad scramble. Attendants rushed me into a small room. It was very cold and had a strong disinfectant smell. Mom wasn't allowed to come in with me. I felt sad and scared. I didn't know what was happening. Why couldn't Mom be with me? I needed her comfort. I wanted to look into her eyes and see her love and support. I wanted to cry out to her, but I couldn't speak. I was never good at hiding or suppressing my emotions. Scared, I cried out to God instead, "Please let me see Mom! Are Mom and Dad okay?" I wanted them to be safe, because then I knew I'd be safe too! After a while, a sense of comfort did come over me. I didn't fully understand it, but God was comforting me.

In the waiting room, the nurses tried to comfort Mom. They spoke to her and got her coffee, and waited with her until Dad arrived. Mom knew something was seriously wrong, but didn't know what. She was frightened and lost in not knowing what was happening.

Back in the room, they cut my swimming trunks off. I was very modest and felt embarrassed. I found out later they asked Mom if she wanted my trunks. Not surprisingly, she passed on their offer. Dad arrived at the hospital during this timeframe. I can't imagine how he made the one hour drive to Rochester with so much unknown going through his mind. When he got there, knowing so little, he wasn't allowed in to see me. Together, my parents were told that I had a spinal cord injury at the C-3 and C-4 cervical vertebrae in my neck—that I was a quadriplegic, meaning all four of my limbs were paralyzed. As if that weren't frightening enough for them, the doctors also told my parents it would be best if they stayed in the hospital overnight because they didn't expect me to live. I still hadn't seen my parents at this point. Mom said her and Dad cried with this news. She said it was like a part of life had been drained from them. They simply held hands and waited to be allowed in to see me.

I, of course, knew nothing about this. While I remember a great deal about the accident, my time in the emergency room is foggy. Perhaps I was sedated. In any case, it's difficult to recall the order in which they did things. I'm sure they put IVs in me, along with other tubes, but I could only feel from my neck up. I do remember them shaving my head, and the doctors drilled tongs in the back of my skull on each side. It sounded like the drills Dad used on the farm. They put weights on the tongs to keep my neck in traction. Even though I had full feeling in my head, I don't remember any pain from this procedure. One of the nurses tried to describe what was being done, but I didn't really understand. I knew something was horribly wrong, but I had no idea that my life had changed drastically, forever. Perhaps because I was too young to understand, I didn't know what was ahead of me. If I had been older, it may have been more than I could handle from an emotional standpoint. Questions like "Why can't I move? Why can't I talk?" ran through my mind. I'm not sure why I never asked them. All I did know was that I needed strength. I prayed, "God help me!" over and over in the emergency room.

There was no reassurance. The staff didn't really talk to me, so I had no idea what was happening. The terminology was like a foreign language. Everyone talked around me and amongst each other. The doctors and nurses looked down at me as they made a surgical incision into my trachea and inserted a curved metal tube into my windpipe. They had gotten permission for the tracheotomy from my parents. Mom was crying when they told her about the need for it. It only confirmed their greatest fears about my condition. The doctors were afraid I would get pneumonia. The tracheotomy would help my lungs drain. I could no longer breathe through my nose or mouth. The only way was through this metal tube. It was, by far, the most painful thing I had to or would endure. After this procedure was finished, they sent me to ICU, and I never saw that group of doctors and nurses again.

They wheeled me from the emergency room on an incredibly loud and squeaky cart, a sound that would later become so familiar that I no longer noticed it. Since the staff didn't communicate with me, I wondered, *Where are they taking me? Can Mom and Dad be with me? Can I go home?*

While the doctors didn't expect me to live through the night, I just thought about going home. I finally got to see Mom and Dad. They knew it might be my last night on earth, but I never sensed that from them. They stayed positive, even though they were torn up inside and hurting from the possibility of losing their son. What good would it do for them to share that sense of panic with me? The answer was, "None." They knew I needed them by my side, that I needed to feel the security of family and home. Mom knew my condition was critical when she saw the tongs in my skull. The last time Dad had seen me was that morning, when we did chores together. A few hours had changed many lives forever. Shockingly, my parents could only stay by my side for the ten minutes allowed by ICU rules in those days. Mom and Dad didn't want to leave, but a nurse ushered them out. This was devastating to my parents and me. I couldn't understand why they had to leave. They went to the chapel and privately prayed for God to spare my life. Something in Mom's heart told her I wouldn't die. Mom visited the chapel many times in the upcoming days. I'm glad I never knew the limits the doctors told my parents. I never once thought I was going to die or be bedridden. I was just going to get better and that was it!

CHAPTER 4
ICU

*"We also rejoice in our sufferings, because we
know that suffering produces perseverance,
perseverance character, and character, hope."*
—Romans 5:3–4

God answered our prayers that night. Though it was touch and go at times, not only did I make it through that night, but I made it through so many more. I wonder what the doctors thought when I was still alive the next morning. From a medical standpoint, they couldn't explain it. Was it a miracle? We think so! Only the long road to recovery shadowed this victory. Little did I know that my life as a quadriplegic had just begun. I went from being a very active twelve-year-old kid to someone who couldn't even move his little finger.

I was in ICU for about a month, and time just dragged on. I could only look up at the ceiling or look at the floor when they turned my bed head over heels to get some air to my back. This was to help prevent bedsores. To pass the time, I'd count the little holes in each section of the ceiling. We used to call my bed "the circle bed" because it performed this procedure. They'd strap a board, not unlike an ironing board, across my chest and sternum so I could be flipped over. This was often awkward as they'd sometimes place the board too high and it would cover my tracheotomy, making it difficult to breathe. Since I couldn't speak, I couldn't yell for help. I felt helpless and afraid. During these times, I cried a lot, but the tears stayed inside. I didn't want anyone seeing them roll down my cheeks. I was living in an unfamiliar world where darkness ruled. I had never felt so much emotional pain. Eventually, I figured out how to put my lips together and quickly pop them open. The resulting popping sound became a way to get the nurse's attention. I felt like a new person every time I learned another way to communicate.

I remember very little of my room. Was there a window? The room seemed so small and always remained a mystery to me. Because of the tongs, I couldn't turn my head to see anything. My bed was close to the door, where I could hear the comings and goings and conversations. I loved the activity of that, but I never felt comfortable there. There was little else to do there. In those days, we didn't have TVs or radios in the hospital. My roommate was an older man. Maybe he was only in his forties or so, but at age twelve, everyone seemed much older. I don't remember much about him, but I can still hear the suctioning from the respirator he had. He moaned in pain, but never talked. No one visited him. My heart ached for him. *He must be so lonely*, I thought. Strange how you can live with someone else for a lengthy time and still not know them or feel familiar with your surroundings.

But the room wasn't the only connection I was missing. I never really had a relationship with the ICU staff. They weren't in my room very much since they could monitor me from their station. Had this been my last night or day on earth, I would have wanted to receive more comfort from them. They should have simply been there for me. Just a caring touch or smile would've been so reassuring. People who are suffering and those at the end of their journey need comfort, hope, compassion, and caring. They need a sense that everything will be okay. How do they get this? From a loving touch, a reassuring smile, or a caring voice. It is this that gives them peace. I never felt any emotion or comfort from my ICU staff.

In fact, I didn't feel much of anything. At this time I still had no feeling from the neck down. I had tubes coming out of me from all directions: my tracheotomy, IVs, a catheter to empty my bladder, oxygen, and others that would come and go depending on what treatment I was being given. The only thing that was painful was the tracheotomy. I never asked about all of the tubes for a couple reasons. First, I didn't know what to ask. Second, I couldn't talk because of the tracheotomy.

That tracheotomy was my only means of breathing for the next five months. The dressing on it was changed daily, sometimes more. Each time, it felt like my throat was being ripped out. The area was extremely tender from the nurses suctioning it out so often. Sometimes, someone would suction too deep and pull that tender skin. It seemed that no sooner would they suction out the mucus and phlegm than it would start building up again. It sounded like the suctioning tube a dentist places in your mouth to get rid of the saliva. Mom and Dad were soon taught how to do this, which was comforting, because when they were with me, they could suction it out as soon as I needed it done. Though I couldn't speak, we later figured out that if I took in a breath and someone put their finger on the tracheotomy, I could talk until the air was used up. Then, they had to quickly remove their finger so I could breathe again. This was quite exhausting, but worth the effort. It was great to have a means of communication again. Months later, they weaned me off the tracheotomy by plugging it up with a cork. Each time, they'd keep it plugged a little longer. I never got used to it. When they finally decided to remove it, I was very scared. What if I can't breathe? I thought. God, please help me breathe! Since my parents couldn't be there, I was even more frightened. But I was able to breathe just fine without it. My prayers had been answered. I could breathe normally again! This was an exhilarating high. None of my worries came to fruition. Later, Mom came to visit. We were both so happy since I could talk again. My voice had changed, since I was going through puberty. It was now quite a bit deeper. I don't remember what my first words were, but I know I didn't shut up.

Overall, the purpose of ICU was to keep me alive and hope I'd stabilize. I wasn't even close to eating at this point. The thought of food was not appealing. I had had a feeding tube in for only a couple weeks, but never knew it because I couldn't yet feel below my neck. Once I had a little bowel results, the feeding tube was removed. I could eat with the trache in, but had no appetite. The indwelling catheter took care of my urine output. As far as the bowels were concerned, they slowly tried to get my body used to a bowel care program. After being given a suppository and waiting for a good half hour, they would insert a finger from a lubricated rubber glove into my bowel and make a circular motion, hoping to stimulate the bowel to move on down. This was repeated several times, but my body had difficulty adjusting. I didn't have any idea what was going on. When I got full surface feeling, only then did I know these cares were being done. It wasn't long before I started to lose my modesty with the nurses and aides.

Time continued to drag on in ICU. All I did was think and count the holes in each ceiling section. I dreamed about getting home and doing chores. I'd go over a daily routine. I just knew I'd be going home soon. It was all about home and family. I still didn't know enough to suspect my life had changed permanently. I thought that once the doctors fixed me, everything would be fine. Whenever I saw my parents, my spirits were lifted. We didn't really talk about my condition, but they gave me hope and a sense of comfort in their presence. Mom and Dad got a room across the street from St. Marys so they could always be close to me. They also formed some strong friendships with family members of other ICU patients. Each day, they were allowed to see me for ten minutes every two hours. This was the highlight of my day. I looked forward to hearing someone walk in. Visitors had to be fifteen years old and immediate family to see me. The only sibling who qualified was Jim. I'll never forget the first time he visited me. Mom had him get close enough to me so I could see his face. The look on his face was innocent, stunned, and unforgettable. Silently, he was asking "What have they done to my brother?" I don't remember him talking. It seemed as though he was in shock. Some of it was his personal sense of guilt.

Years later, Jim confessed, "Randy, when you floated up face down, I thought you were joking around, so when I got to you I dunked your head back down in the water. When you floated back up, I realized you were really hurt. I have always wondered if I made your injury worse!"

"You didn't hurt me any worse," I said. "The damage was done when I entered the water! If it wasn't for you, I never would've survived!"

It was never Jim's fault. The doctors said the injury resulted from me taking the full impact of the dive on the top of my head. It was simply a freak accident. But I felt terrible for Jim.

"For years," he said, "I've awakened in cold sweats having nightmares about the accident."

"But you've allowed me to live a great life!" I told him, gratefully. Jim was always a good big brother. Carrying that guilt around with him must have been horrible.

As always, at the end of any visit from family, I wondered, *When will I see them again?* I hated when the ten minute visitations were up. It meant I had two more hours to wait. All I could think about was home! It filled me with hope.

That hope was something I hung onto for the next year and a half, the time I spent in the hospital. Originally the doctors had told my parents I wouldn't live through the first night, but I did. Then, they said I wouldn't survive the next few days, but I did. Next, they said I'd be bedridden, but I'm not. Finally, they gave me a life expectancy of fifteen years—forty-five years ago.

We put our trust and lives in the hands of doctors, and I was fortunate to have some of the best doctors in the world, but Mom, Dad, and I believed it was God who had the final say.

CHAPTER 5
PRIVATE ROOM

"But the fruit of the Spirit is love, joy, peace, patience, kindness, goodness, faithfulness."
—Galatians 5:22

When my condition had stabilized, I was moved to a private room on the second floor. The room was bigger and much brighter. This room, I came to know. Here, I could see my parents throughout the day during the entire visiting hour span. That brightened my spirits more than anything. Mom, who worked at the Hormel meat packing plant in Austin, Minnesota, had taken an unpaid leave to be with me as much as possible. My parents had given up their room across the street, and Mom drove over to see me every day.

My three youngest siblings were staying with grandparents, aunts and uncles, and friends. Jim was a young man during the summer of 1966. He stayed on the farm and, with the help of uncles and neighbors, he did the chores and kept the farm going. The farm community had been in action while Dad was away. The neighbor farmers had planted the rest of the soybeans. But there was still so much work to be done. Dad had to start spending more time back home on the farm. Dad was there as much as he could be. Whenever he came, he stayed quite a while. But when it was time to leave, he had the same ritual. He always made sure he was the last one out the door, and he'd turn back toward me and say, "Keep your chin up!" Not sure what it was about those words, but it made me feel as if everything would be okay.

In the beginning of my hospitalization, the doctors had encouraged Mom and Dad to put me in an institution where they thought I could get the best therapy and schooling, but my parents wanted nothing to do with that. "Absolutely not," they said. "He's going home with us to be a member of our family again." They never thought twice about it. The institution was never an option.

Financially, I have no idea how they managed. Clearly, God was in control. It was no coincidence that my family was surrounded by wonderful relatives and friends. Since my three youngest siblings were scattered among them, they handled the expenses for the children. Everyone told my parents not to worry about finances. The department Mom worked at in the Hormel plant took up a collection and sent it to my parents. Dad still had a milk check coming in since Jim, uncles, and neighbors milked the cows. Perhaps the biggest burden endured by all was to have the security of family uprooted. The hospital staff warned my parents that an accident like this could tear a family apart and be very hard on a marriage. My parents never let that change their thoughts about our family bond. They believed the accident could bring us closer together as a family—that it might make us stronger as we helped each other out.

Needless to say, my favorite part of the day was when Mom and Dad came to see me. Mom faithfully came every day. My spirits soared when I heard her footsteps in the hall! She read my mail to me. I got tons of letters and cards from family, friends, relatives, teachers, classmates, 4-H members, and many others. These messages were filled with so much love and support. Folks wanted me to know I was in their thoughts and prayers. They all hoped I'd get well soon. It was inspiring! Mom taped them to the wall and on my bed. When my 4-H club sent me a long letter, I had Mom write a letter back saying I'd be home soon to help out the softball team. We'd won the county championship two years earlier. This year, we had another good team. It must have been hard for Mom to write that letter when she knew in her heart I would likely never throw a softball again. Still, she never discouraged me.

It was here that I also started looking forward to seeing others and developing friendships. Two of my favorite new friends were a nurse and an aide. Judy was a blonde nurse, short in stature, and with a gentle voice. Brad, an aide, was a jokester who lightened the load whenever I saw him. "Hey, big guy! How are you today?" he'd ask each time he entered the room. He grew up about twenty miles from me in a small, north Iowa town, giving us lots in common. I loved Brad and Judy. They always seemed to have time for me. Whenever one of them was on duty, I knew it would be a good day!

The support of friends and family meant a great deal to me as the real work began. Physical therapy sessions were held in my room. Different therapists gave me normal range therapy—stretching my arms and legs to keep the muscles from tightening. These sessions lasted about fifteen minutes or so, only growing more intense when I was able to sit up and go down to the therapy unit. Those sessions lasted forty-five to sixty minutes.

Every morning, the doctors would come in and prick me with a straight pin. At first, I had no feeling from my neck down, but eventually, I started to feel the pin prick in my chest. I'll never forget the sense of excitement! I couldn't wait to tell Mom and Dad. As time went on, I could feel the prick all the way down to my toes. I had developed surface feeling, not deep feeling. This means I can feel touch throughout my body, but can't differentiate if I'm being touched with something cold or hot, sharp or dull. For instance, I can feel a nurse give me an injection, but don't feel the pain. If I get the flu, I have stomach pain like anyone else. I remember once when I was on rehab, one of the aides turned me on my side and my hand flopped over to my private area. I asked, "Why does it feel so rough there?"

Mom said, "You now have hair down there." I never felt so embarrassed in my life! Mom and the aide made no big deal about it. It was dropped and never brought up again. Many people assume paralysis means no feeling. Since my spinal cord isn't severed, this is not the case with me. This explains why I have touch feeling. I wouldn't have any feeling with a severed spinal cord. This starts about chest level.

Eventually, the doctors felt I no longer needed to be in traction. They removed the tongs and placed a brace on me. The brace fit down over my shoulders, up under my chin, and up the back of my head. I was still very restricted in movement, but thrilled to have the tongs out—particularly after a memorable incident when they actually fell out. I'd been in my new room for a week or two when Judy, my favorite nurse, was there to help. She placed her hands behind my head and held it as still as possible. All this time, she was leaning over my bed in an awkward position. She said to me with the sweetest smile, "Don't worry, Randy, everything will be just fine!" Then she said, "I'm right here and will hold your head still until the doctor comes."

Her gentle voice calmed my fears! I wasn't afraid or worried in her presence. I simply said, "Thank you!" She smiled. There was so much compassion and love in her voice. I'm sure this was a difficult situation for her too, but I never sensed it. When the doctor got there, he shaved my head and drilled the tongs back in place.

Then, I got to the point where I could sit up a bit once I had the brace on. The first time I sat up was only for a couple minutes because I got very lightheaded and nearly fainted. I hadn't been in a sitting position for many weeks. The blood rushed from my head. My physical therapist knew this would be a strong possibility. He was on the lookout for it.

"Do you feel okay?" he asked.

I didn't want to say, no, so I tried to last a bit longer, but finally gave in, and they put me back in bed. It may have only been a couple minutes, but another obstacle had been conquered. This slowly got better as time went on. Eventually, I got to the point where they decided I no longer needed the brace. I'll never forget the strange feeling I experienced the first time I sat up without the brace. I was so used to neck support that it felt like my head would literally fall off. This got better with time and therapy. Learning how to sit up and use a wheelchair were accomplishments that gave me a great deal more independence. They were significant milestones to my parents, therapists, doctors, nurses, and me.

CHAPTER 6
EATING

"Each one must give as he has decided
in his heart, not reluctantly
or under compulsion, for God
loves a cheerful giver."
—2 Corinthians 9:7

After my accident, I didn't eat anything for quite a while. They let me try Jell-o after a few weeks. I'll never forget it. It was red and cut in cubes. I didn't like the taste. I had no appetite. It was difficult getting used to chewing and swallowing while lying flat on my back. The thought of eating was revolting. I lost thirty pounds during the first part of my hospital stay. But they pushed the Jell-o over and over. Each time, I would try it and spew red vomit through my mouth and tracheotomy. Needless to say, it made quite a mess. The nurses didn't seem to mind cleaning it up. To this day, I can't stand the thought of eating Jell-o. But it was part of the process.

It took a while for my body to accept eating again. Eventually, I got my appetite back and enjoyed eating. I couldn't eat much at first but was consuming normal portions soon after my appetite returned. For some reason, though, I never got my appetite for breakfast back. I'd give mine to my roommate. Seems we always had soft boiled eggs, and they only seemed half cooked to me. They had that snotty consistency that was so unappealing. In those days, you typically ate what they brought you. There wasn't a choice in the hospital. After being there for months, the food began to taste the same—didn't matter if it was ham or hamburger.

In any case, I had to be fed. I loved it when Mom fed me. She knew the pace I liked to eat at. When the aides fed me, some shoveled it in fast and others extremely slow. Some fed me small bites, some big bites, and some just the right size. I didn't get fed until the food trays were passed out to all the patients. Sometimes, I had to wait. On days they were short staffed, sometimes an aide would start to feed me and, between bites, would help someone else by cutting up his meat, pouring his coffee, opening a sugar packet, or whatever else was needed. Many times, the food was cold, but at least someone cared enough to help me.

What I could hardly wait for was home cooking. Grandma, Mom's mom, came with Mom once a week to visit when I got to the rehab wing. She always brought lemon meringue pie that she'd baked in a little pot pie tin. Grandma knew this was my favorite desert. And she always brought two, so my roommate could have one. "Thanks, Grandma!" I'd say enthusiastically.

"Hope you enjoy it," she'd say. "I'll bring you another one next week." She always did, too. Grandma looked a lot like Mom, but I, of course, thought she looked a lot older. She had gray hair and a smile that glowed. Mom was a much younger version of Grandma. It's clear where she got her looks and her ways. As kids, we loved staying overnight at my grandparents' place. They made it special. We knew Grandma would fix our favorite food. Grandpa was a carpenter, and I loved going into his shop. I can still smell that freshly cut wood. They had rows and rows of raspberry bushes. Grandpa had us pick lots of those raspberries. He'd give us a quarter for helping. We thought that was a big deal. Grandma made different kinds of jams and desserts out of those raspberries. Everything she made tasted great. They took us to some of their friends' places, and we loved listening to their stories.

Grandma's visit always brought that level of comfort. And, as with the lemon meringue pies, she brought comfort in many forms. When

I was able to sit up in my wheelchair, Grandma and Mom would both scratch my scalp with a brush. Grandma had this certain brush she kept in her purse. She would brush my scalp and get rid of the dry skin. It felt so good. Since I was in bed so much, I always got a dry scalp. This became a ritual between Grandma and me even after I got out of the hospital.

Little things in life took on a whole new meaning to me. Eating is an essential part of life, and I couldn't eat anything unless someone fed it to me. I learned to cherish the kind acts of others who helped me. When the Israelites were led by Moses out of slavery from Egypt, they complained about nearly everything instead of being thankful (Exodus 12:31).

Dad always said, "You don't have to look far to see someone who is worse off than you." That's how I felt in the hospital. I learned to appreciate things because one look around and you could always find someone in worse shape.

CHAPTER 7
I WONDERED

"I will instruct you and teach you in the way you should go; I will counsel you with my eye upon you."
—Psalm 32:8

When I'd been in the hospital about three weeks, I started to let my mind wander after my parents had left and the daily activities were done. The evenings seemed so long. I wondered about my friends at school. I had broken my neck just days before the end of sixth grade. What were my friends doing? I received letters from them, so I knew they knew about my accident. I figured they were busy with summer activities, such as swimming, playing ball, staying with friends, fishing, and more. I wondered about my sixth grade teacher. She was one of my favorites. She was kind to every student, and she knew just how far to push each of us to get us to excel. Sixth grade marked the end of elementary school, which meant I'd start junior high school the next year. Little did I know that I wouldn't be going with my friends to seventh grade.

I wondered about the 4-H softball team. I had practiced with them just two days before my accident. The team members were really nice. Many of them were neighbors. Plus, I'd always shown sheep at the county fair, but this year I was going to show a beef calf. I knew it needed to be worked with so it would be ready for the fair in early August. I wondered about our farm animals. Who was doing the chores

I used to do? How was our dog, Major, doing? I missed him. He was a beautiful collie who would even play football with us. We'd start running with a football, and Major would run after us, tackling us by wrapping his paws around our waists.

And the crops, I wondered how they were doing. It was just past the middle of June. The farmers had a saying that corn should be knee high by the fourth of July, which was true at the time before fertilizers and chemicals led to early maturation. Dad used to say to us kids, "Be quiet and listen for a few seconds." When we were, he'd ask, "Do you hear the corn growing?" He always sounded serious too. Sometimes, I was sure I did hear it growing.

By now, I thought, Dad was probably busy cultivating the corn and bean crops. We usually baled hay in later June or early July. If the weather cooperated, we could get a second crop of hay later in the summer. It always seemed to be the hottest part of the summer when we hayed. Dad said haying was the hardest work on the farm. After it was baled in the field, the elevator would bring it up, and we stacked it in the hayloft. It was always so hot up there!

One night, after we'd worked hard baling and stacking hay, Dad asked, "Are you tired tonight?"

I answered with an exhausted, "Yeah!"

"It's a good tired, isn't it?" he asked.

"I guess so," I replied. Back then, I wasn't sure what he meant by that, but as I got older, I realized it meant it felt good to work so hard and have a lot accomplished at day's end. I knew those lessons of hard work on the farm were helping me make it through therapy.

I also wondered about our vegetable garden. We'd planted a large garden that spring. I found myself spending lots of time in the garden. I couldn't wait to see how the plants changed day to day. I even enjoyed weeding it because it made the garden look clean and fresh. I liked that sense of accomplishment. Mom did lots of canning in those days. We ate a variety of fresh vegetables too. They tasted so good. Mom was a very good cook and mixed in fresh vegetables with every meal.

Although that garden was a lot of work, it kept me close to nature. I often thought back to the beauty of the farm. I always loved to see and hear the miracles God had waiting outside each morning—from the birds singing to the sun rising in the east. The sounds and sights were so beautiful. There is something about the charm of nature that is therapeutic and peaceful. The memories served me well.

I wondered what my siblings were doing. Did they go fishing and swimming at the six mile grove? We used to go there nearly every Saturday in the summer. We'd put the fish we caught in the cow tank, and they'd live a long time. The cow tank was filled regularly to provide water for the cows to drink. Was Jim working and doing chores on the farm? Was Becky out in the playhouse? She used to spend hours out there. Did Bob and Linda go down to the railroad tracks and try to catch pollywogs in the creek under the tracks? The pollywogs would turn into frogs. Did they catch caterpillars and watch the cocoons turn into butterflies? So many of God's miracles surrounded us. We all did these things and couldn't wait to show Mom and Dad.

I often fell asleep after my wondering sessions. It became a means of escape from the unfamiliar surroundings of the hospital. Just thinking about my life at home took me right back to that familiar place. When I was growing up, the family really was a unit of one. We shared every triumph and failure. Security and support was what family meant. Just the memories helped me cope each day.

CHAPTER 8
PITY PARTY

*"In your anger do not sin; do not let
the sun go down on your anger."*
—Ephesians 4:26

I remember July 4, 1966, very clearly. It marked five weeks in the hospital. I was still in the private room on the second floor, and it was becoming quite apparent that my hospital stay was going to last much longer than I had originally believed. I wasn't feeling good about this. In fact, I was downright blue. I didn't want to celebrate Fourth of July in the hospital. Fourth of July and the county fair were always the two highlights of the Krulish family summer. Lyle might have been a small town, but its people sure knew how to have a celebration. People came from miles around to enjoy the parade, the kid's games, bingo, good food, and many other events. And the day was capped off with a beautiful display of fireworks! The thought of missing this celebration made me depressed.

Nothing could cheer me up. On the Fourth, Mom, Dad, and Jim came to visit me. Mom had even made a special picnic lunch, though I wasn't eating much yet. It was a typical thoughtful Mom act. Dad picked up on my attitude right away. He decided it was time to have a talk with me.

"Look Randy," he said. "We're sorry you have to be in the hospital too! This is the only place that will make you better so you can come home. We tried to make this day as special for you as we could. You're not showing much appreciation by acting this way. Even though it may not seem like it, you have a lot to be thankful for. It's time to change your attitude. With this kind of attitude, you'll never get better."

Just hearing him lecture me, however well intentioned, hurt a lot. And it hit home. I had tears in my eyes because I was sad and down, but I never responded because I knew he was right. I'm very sensitive, and words can easily hurt me. What Dad said that day hurt, but he said it out of love. He wasn't insensitive and harsh. He wanted what was best for me. Basically, in no uncertain terms, he gave me a quick attitude adjustment. Did I like it? No. Was it best for me? Most definitely! It wasn't easy for him either. He just knew it was something he had to say. He also knew I needed to hear it, like it or not. It wouldn't have been good for me had he just empathized and felt sorry for me. It would've only deepened my negative attitude and validated my terrible frame of mind. I didn't need any more fuel for that fire. Instead, Dad saw I needed a wakeup call, and he gave it to me. It took great love on Dad's part to say what he did, considering my condition. The love of a parent is one of the most powerful things there is. That day, Dad showed me firsthand what that love is all about. It's not necessarily doing what you want to do, but it's about doing what is right and best for your children.

His lecture stuck with me always. I'd often replay it when I felt blue. It proved to be a great pick-me-up for the rest of my hospital stay and my life. When Dad finished his lecture, it was quiet in the room for a couple of minutes. Jim didn't breathe a word. We kids knew to be quiet and listen when Dad talked. Finally, Mom cheerfully said, "Let's have a picnic!" The day turned into a pretty good one considering the circumstances. We shared some family memories and much needed laughter.

CHAPTER 9
I KNEW

"Think over what I say, for the Lord will give you understanding in everything."
—2 Timothy 2:7

When my parents asked the doctors what they should tell me about my accident, they were told to either tell me everything or wait until I asked. Mom and Dad decided to wait until I asked, thinking I would be ready to hear it then. They never told me that I broke my neck and, as a result, was a quadriplegic. And I never asked!

It wasn't until I was moved to the rehab wing of First East that I first heard the words *broken neck.* One of the aides mentioned it in a passing conversation with another staff member. My ears perked up for a second. Then, my thoughts continued on with what I was doing. Those words only confirmed what I already knew. Sometimes we simply know things without having to be told.

Today, psychologists are available in the hospital to help people deal with a life-changing accident like mine. It gives you an outlet for your feelings, someone to talk to and answer your questions. This was not the case when I broke my neck. I just learned by osmosis in a sense. The rehab wing was on the first floor, the east wing of the hospital. There, I was surrounded by paraplegics and other quadriplegics. When I was there, I just knew.

I never asked anyone what had happened, maybe because I was afraid of the answer. If I didn't hear it, then it wasn't reality. Over the years, many people have said, "Bet you wished you hadn't gone swimming that day." I never thought that way. And I never regretted making that dive. If it was meant to be it would've happened no matter what I was doing that day. The only thing I did wonder was, *What did I do that was so bad to deserve this?* The only thing I could recall was something that happened when my cousin stayed overnight once. My dad was a smoker, and we collected some of his cigarette butts and tried lighting them and smoking them. We were terrible at it, and I hated the taste. I didn't understand the attraction. We just wanted to be cool! And I had friends who had done many worse things than I had. In many ways, I didn't think the accident was fair to me. I didn't think it would be fair to anyone. It was just a few moments of wondering, *Why me?* I was never comfortable believing that God wanted this for me. Many things happen that we just don't understand. And this was one of them.

CHAPTER 10
THE COUNTY FAIR

"Let all that you do be done in love."
—1 Corinthians 16:14

I moved to First East at the end of July, marking two months in the hospital. The staff packed my stuff, placed it on an old wooden cart, and wheeled me to my new home, the place where I would work hard on physical and occupational therapies. At this point, I still had my neck brace on for support and the tracheotomy in, and I was barely eating anything. I was only sitting up for a few minutes at a time. Working more on the therapies to gain new skills and independence was both exciting and anxiety inducing, knowing it was a step closer to going home, yet it also meant getting to know new staff members and other patients. It was hard saying good-bye to Judy and Brad. They touched my life with their love and compassion in a way that I'll never forget.

Soon after the move, as I was meeting the staff and fellow patients, my parents gave me some exciting news. They had talked with my head doctor on First East, Dr. Jackson, and gotten permission for me to go see my calf being judged at the Mower County Fair in Austin, about an hour from the hospital. I was thrilled! This was just days away. I figured time would go by slowly, but it didn't because I was busy getting used to the new routine, going to therapy, and meeting my therapists. But during my down time, all I could think of was the fair. I would finally get to see the rest of my brothers and sisters, and probably some friends from school and 4-H too. I couldn't wait. "Thank you, God!" I exclaimed.

The night before my trip to the fair was a long one. I was awake most of the night. I knew the Mower County Fair was only six miles from my home on the farm, and I really wanted to go there.

"Can I go home for just a few minutes?" I asked.

"Sorry," said Dad, "but Dr. Jackson only okayed enough time to go to the fair and back."

Although I was disappointed, just going to the fair and getting away from the hospital for a spell was enticing. My Uncle Bob, Mom's only sibling, the fireman who was at the lake the day of my accident, had worked out the details so he could transport me by ambulance. Dr. Jackson understood the importance of therapy, but he also knew the importance of having high spirits and approaching therapy in the proper frame of mind. He was a man of few words, but a very wise man.

When it was time to go, the staff placed me on an ambulance cot and wheeled me to the emergency room garage. It felt great to feel the fresh, outdoor air again. "Have fun!" shouted one of the aides. I knew I would. It had been about nine weeks since my accident, and I was ready. They placed me in the ambulance, and my uncle drove off to the fair. Mom and Dad were there for the ride. I remember the smiles on their faces. They knew the psychological boost this would give me. The drive didn't take as long as I thought it would. On the way, my parents and I talked about who would be there. When we pulled into the fairgrounds, Uncle Bob drove right up to the 4-H judging pavilion. He and Dad pulled me out of the ambulance, and into the pavilion we went. I'll never forget the warmth of the sun on my face as they pulled me out of the ambulance. It had been over two months since I felt direct sunshine. The last sun I had felt was lying on that beach after breaking my neck. That was a moment of fear and confusion. This was a moment of thanksgiving.

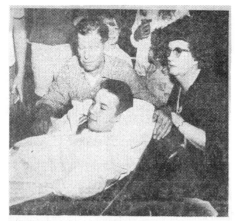

RANDY AND PARENTS VIEW 4-H BEEF SHOW

4-H Boy Comes by Ambulance to See Entry Judged at Fair

Randy Krulish, 12, son of Mr. and Mrs. Frank L. Krulish Jr., Austin Rt. 2, saw his lightweight Angus steer judged Tuesday morning after an ambulance ride from St. Marys Hospital, Rochester.

Showing for his first year in 4-H beef competition at the Mower County Fair, he received a red ribbon.

Thanks to the Enterprise 4-H Club, of which he is a member, Randy had the most fun he's had since that fateful Memorial Day when joy was turned to sorrow as he suffered two broken vertabrae in a swimming accident near Faribault. He has been hospitalized ever since.

Randy had showed sheep in the past, but this was his first year with a beef project. His calf which he showed Tuesday was born May, 1965, and Randy cared for him for a year with the fair in mind. Randy has been a 4-Her four years.

Randy's mother and a registered nurse rode in the ambulance with him. A special apparatus was made available at Crane Pavilion. Randy had a tracheotomy following his ac-

cident, and the nurse had to watch carefully to see that his breathing was okay.

When his steer went into the ring, Randy was placed on a stretcher at ringside. His brother, Jim, 15, who is showing sheep and pigs, brought the steer into the ring.

After the show, Randy returned to Rochester where he is having therapy.

In summing up the trip to Austin for the beef show, his mother said the doctor at Rochester said, "It's better than any medicine we could give him."

Mom, Dad, and me at the county fair (1966)

When we got to the pavilion, I saw my siblings right away. They all had smiles on their faces and were waving at me. I was relieved to see they looked the same. I'm sure my parents had explained to them what to expect when they saw me. I knew Jim knew what to expect since I'd seen him a couple times. Becky was now eleven, and she still had her long, blonde hair. Bob and Linda looked exactly the same at six and three respectively. Bob and Linda would later only recall bits and pieces of this time because of how young they were. For me, the moment held great comfort because I could see they were still the same. That feeling of family security came rushing back.

I was greeted by a chorus of "Hi, Randy!" wherever I went. But something in the way they looked at me, and the sound of hesitancy in their voices, didn't feel right. They were confused and didn't know what to expect. One classmate just stared at me. He didn't wave or say a word to me. His shocked and confused demeanor really stuck with me. But thankfully, I didn't have much time to think about it. It was time for my calf to be judged. Jim and the father of another 4-H member showed my calf. He acted up quite a bit by kicking and jumping, and was hesitant about being led around for show, which was understandable considering he hadn't been worked with much during the summer. In the end, I got a red ribbon, which is in the second place grouping. Previously, I'd gotten all blue ribbons when showing my sheep, but I wasn't going to let that ruin my excitement. The judge brought the ribbon to me and handed it to Dad. I knew we still had some time before we had to head back to the hospital, and I wanted to soak up every experience I could.

"Do you want to try sitting up for a bit?" Mom and Dad asked.

"Sure!"

Although Dad could just pick me up by himself, my Uncle Bob helped him place me in my chair. Mom adjusted the positioning so it was most comfortable. She knew the little nuances that felt best for me.

"What do you want to eat?" was the next question. Mom said I could have any fair food I wanted. Of all of the funnel cakes and corn dogs and other delicious fair food, for some reason, I wanted a hamburger. So, they got me one across the street from the pavilion. I only ate a few bites, but it was enough. It tasted amazing after weeks of hospital food.

Time was running out. I was getting tired from sitting up. Soon Dad said, "We better get ready to go back to the hospital." I was disappointed but was also ready to lie back down on the ambulance cot. Dad and Uncle Bob lifted me onto the cot. Before they put me in the ambulance, my brothers and sisters gathered around to say their good-byes. I was sad knowing I had to leave them. In the ambulance, I asked once more, "Can we go home for just a minute?" I knew the answer, but had to try.

Dad said, "Sorry, we have to get back." I had an empty feeling inside me while heading back to the hospital. Mom and Dad filled the time talking about what we did and whom we saw. This helped ease the pain. I was disappointed, but knew my battery had been recharged. I wanted to work hard in therapy so I could go home sooner. That was my only goal: get home! Back on First East, the staff got me settled into my hospital bed. They were happy for me and asked questions about my day. Mom hung the red ribbon on my bed. All of this, and the memories of the day, put me back in a positive frame of mind. My parents and Dr. Jackson had just given me a taste of home. I wanted more.

CHAPTER 11
MY FAMILY ON FIRST EAST

*"Rejoice in hope, be patient in
tribulation, be constant in prayer."*
—Romans 12:12

Fortunately for me, the atmosphere on First East was much more like family. It was exactly what someone who was craving home needed. The room was a dark green color. Not exactly bright and cheerful, but it was my home away from home. It was a small, double room with barely enough room for two beds. My wheelchair and cart were parked in the hallway outside the room. As for hospital rules, they were more relaxed here too. The nurses and aides didn't care if a visitor stayed past visiting hours.

But First East was not a quiet location. The hall was a constant source of noise. The wheels on the carts all seemed to squeak. The med cart had a stop and go sound as they wheeled it from room to room. Even the catheter team cart made a big lumbering sound when it came by so the staff could change and irrigate my catheter. I didn't mind that sound, though, because the staff was always friendly and cheerful. Once a week, at 5:00 a.m., I could hear that scale coming all the way from the next wing. It made a grinding metal sound as it moved across the floor. And then there was the supply cart. Every morning, a man with a huge cart would stick his head in the door and holler, "Newspapers!" He sold soda pop and toothpaste to candy bars and so much more. I hardly ever bought anything, but Mom would let me have a pop once in a while.

There was always something happening on First East. Once a month, a kind lady would swing by our room with a cart full of different artwork. She'd ask if we wanted a new one for our wall. We always agreed. The pictures were scenic and a welcome change. And there were always footsteps in the hall. After a while, I was able to distinguish everyone by their tread, whether nurses, aides, doctors, therapists, or visitors.

Many of the people I met on First East became close friends, bound together by our life-changing experiences. My friends ranged in age from twelve to sixty, with varying degrees of paralysis. I found so much inspiration in each of them. My first roommate, Eric, was my age. He had been in the pediatrics unit, but they moved him to First East after I arrived. Eric had polio. Many surgeries and significant therapy were ahead of him. Since we were both long term patients, it was a perfect match. We became best friends and shared everything. We lived together for months to come and became so close that we still correspond today. Our mothers became close too.

The girl who lived in the room next to me, Julie, was eighteen. She broke her back in a car accident and became a paraplegic. She planned to go to nursing school to follow her dream of becoming a registered nurse. Before her accident, she had a steady boyfriend. After, he visited her in the hospital and decided she was no longer a "complete" woman. He left her. We felt sad for her. But she never let it slow her down. That was inspiring. She brought laughter to the halls of First East with her sparkling personality and sense of humor. Julie was so positive that it rubbed off on me. Eventually, she did get her nursing degree and married a doctor. I went to her wedding, and we've remained friends.

Another patient I became close to was Paul, a man in his twenties who was a quadriplegic but could still use his arms quite a bit. I could relate to Paul because he was a farmer. He was determined to continue working the farm in whatever capacity he could. When he went home, he had his tractor adapted so he could work out in the fields.

Zach, who had polio, was completely paralyzed and lived in an iron lung that looked like a big green tube stretching from his feet to his neck. This helped him breathe. His arms stuck out the side and just lay alongside the iron lung. He had huge hands. And the only way he could see anything was when he looked up into a mirror that had been placed above his head. There, he could see through the reflection in the mirror, although everything he saw was backward. I couldn't imagine what life was like for him. It seemed so unfair and difficult. But Zach was so used to it that it was second nature to him. I remember what a fantastic chess player he was. We played many times. He was virtually unbeatable, which is remarkable since the chess board and chess pieces he saw were backward to him. He always had a smile on his face.

One such unforgettable soul was Tom, who was a bit of a lower level quad than I. He could move his arms a bit, but not his fingers. He was soft spoken and always had a Bible on his lap. He flopped his hand down by the corner of the page, caught his thumbnail under the page, and then tried to turn it. Sometimes, this would take him several tries and many minutes. I watched in amazement because he was kind and patient, and he had a glow about him that was something I wanted and needed. Little did I know, but this helped the seed of God already in me begin to grow more. Tom was probably thirty or forty years old. He became a quadriplegic when he and his wife were in a car accident. He broke his neck in the accident, but his wife escaped without a scratch. When he got to First East, she left him and their eight children. She decided she no longer wanted to be a wife or mother. What consoled him and gave him the strength to go on was his Bible. Reading it eased his pain and gave him peace. I lost touch with him shortly after I left the hospital. Last I knew, he was living with his sister, and they were raising his children together. But he gave me an unending gift: witnessing the joy that can come from God. He touched my life in a powerful way.

My fellow patients, like me, had their lives changed forever by their accidents. One thing they all had in common, though, was the drive and determination to make something out of their new lives. I wanted to follow their lead. It gave me the strength to go on.

CHAPTER 12
THE DAILY ROUTINE

"Come to me, all who labor, and are
heavy laden, and I will give you rest."
—Matthew 11:28

There was no time for boredom on First East. Our day started bright and early when the nurse came at 7:30 a.m. to take our vitals, blood pressure, and temperature. I was always awake when she came in, woken by the shift change at 7:00 a.m. Then came breakfast, which I never ate. This was followed by our daily cares, like bed bath, which consisted of an aide filling up a wash basin and washing my whole body from head to toe with a wash cloth and towel. I never felt completely clean from this bath. A bath blanket was placed under me before the bath. When it was time to wash my back, the aide would grab the first available staff member to help turn me on my side. Sometimes this would take a few minutes. When I could sit up more in my wheelchair, showering was another tricky task to learn, and one that made me face my fears directly. They transferred me on a plastic shower chair, wrapped me in a bath blanket that never seemed to fully cover me, and took me down to the shower room. This was just a short distance from my room. I never liked being wheeled to the shower room. I felt exposed. The first time, I wasn't sure what to expect, but when the aide removed the bath blanket, I felt so embarrassed. There I was, naked, with a female aide in the shower room. She was just doing her job and never made a big deal out of it. It got easier as time went on. But when she turned the water on and pointed the shower head in my face, I wanted to yell, "Stop!" The day of my accident came rushing back. The spray of the water in my face was very much like that suffocating feeling of floating up, facedown, in the lake. I struggled to breathe as I filled with anxiety and panic! The aide pointed the shower head elsewhere until I could once again breathe. I never shared this fear with any aide or my parents. I'm not sure why I kept so much inside. The air felt precious, just as it did when Jim turned me over in the lake. It took me a long time to adjust to the showers, but eventually, I started to look forward to them. I'd have a shower every day if time allowed.

Next was the bowel care program, catheter care, getting dressed, and more. My catheter, designed to keep urine draining from my bladder, was changed every couple weeks. This involved inserting tubing into my bladder through the penis. Then, a small plastic ball was inflated with about 10 ccs of saline solution. This kept the catheter from coming out. Then, the long catheter tubing drained into a large bag attached to the side of my bed. Proper care helped keep me from getting urinary tract infections. First East was nice because we could wear regular clothes, as if we were home. This restored some normalcy in my life. It felt strange having someone else put my clothes on me, though. I felt helpless, but I always believed everything would be normal when I got home.

Cheerful nurses' aides handled all of my cares. I had two favorites who were in their early twenties: Jill and Nancy. Both were kind, caring, and had great senses of humor. I remember Jill, who was blonde to Nancy's dark hair, in particular. She always asked how it was going, would tell me what time my therapies were scheduled, and would ask if I needed anything. She was easy to talk to and was always happy to help. She'd ask, "Is your mom coming today?" She knew how Mom's visits brightened my day. Jill even talked about the weather and kept me connected with the outside world, from which I had long been separated. She gave me a tiny bottle of cologne on my thirteenth birthday in December 1966. It was beautifully wrapped. And, when she opened it for me, she said, "You're a teenager now, and you can wear some cologne." I thanked her for the gift, but felt a bit embarrassed because it recognized my changing body and adolescence. I don't think I ever wore it, but that didn't lessen its significance. It was a gesture I'll never forget. Little kind acts like this helped me get through those days on First East.

The aides on First East worked hard to get all of our cares done in time for therapy. Sometime in the early morning hours, the doctor and his student doctors would stop to check on us. Dr. Jackson was a highly respected physical medicine and rehabilitation physician. He was a relatively quiet man, so each morning was the same. He'd ask how I was, and I'd always respond with, "Fine." The student doctors with him were learning the ropes of rehab, so he often explained what he was doing and discussed terminology with them. During the exam, Dr. Jackson would touch me in various places, from shoulders to toes, and ask, "Can you feel me touch you?"

By this time, I had almost full surface feeling back, so I'd answer, "Yeah." Eventually, he'd be more specific. "Which toe am I touching?" he'd ask.

I'd answer accordingly and never got any wrong. One day after going through this same ritual, he said, "I'd say you have full surface feeling back." This made me feel so proud. I thanked him with enthusiasm. He then put his hand on top of my shoulder and asked, "Can you shrug your shoulder?" At first I couldn't, but as time went on, I could shrug some. This was thanks to the hard work of physical therapy. Then, he'd push down on my shoulders and say, "Now, try shrugging them." This was harder, but he always said, "Good job."

Weeks later, he'd try holding my arm out and say, "Try pulling your arm in." I'd make an effort, and he'd stop me, saying, "No, you're using your shoulder muscles. Try using your arm muscles." I'd try again, with the same results. "We'll try again tomorrow," he'd say. Moments like this made me frustrated and disappointed in a way that's hard to describe. I tried so hard to move a certain muscle, but the thought could no longer pass through to my brain because of the spinal cord injury. Other muscles, shoulder muscles, would take over.

We also had daily occupational and physical therapy, we called them OT and PT. The times of our therapies were listed on a card outside our door. We had two sessions of PT, one in the morning and one in the afternoon. OT was only once a day, usually in the morning.

When it was time for lunch, we headed to the dining room. We could have breakfast in our rooms, but lunch and dinner were required to be eaten in the dining room. There were exceptions to this, including not feeling well or having visitors. Most of us preferred the dining room because it was bigger and brighter than our rooms, with huge windows that let the sunshine inside. It was a nice break from the daily routine. The dining room was a gathering place with lots of tables. Each had room for four wheelchairs, and we could sit at any one that was available. I had many friends, so I always found someone to sit next to. We usually talked about our food, therapy, and family. It was a time of fellowship.

After an aide would clamp off my catheter and help the attendant get me on the cart, so I could go to therapy. The therapy wing wasn't too far down the hall from First East. Once, when I returned from the two therapy sessions, I started feeling chilly and clammy, and had a pounding headache. Mom could tell something was wrong, and she got Jill to check me out. As it turned out, they had never reconnected my catheter to the bed bag. It had been clamped off much longer than it should've been. My bladder was screaming to be emptied. After that, whenever I felt like that, I knew something was probably pinched off with my catheter.

Sorting through the many emotions during my hospital stay was complicated. Some were exhilarating, some downright unpleasant. But each created something to learn from and each was a part of my journey.

CHAPTER 13
BEING TUTORED

"A disciple is not above his teacher, but everyone, when he is fully trained, will be like his teacher."
—Luke 6:40

The end of August marked three months in the hospital. Back home, school was about to start. My roommate made plans for tutors to come to the hospital so he could start seventh grade. Since we were the same age and in the same grade, it only made sense that I should be tutored with him. By this time, it was very apparent that I wouldn't go to school with my classmates. No one ever said this, but it was clear I had significant therapy yet and my hospital stay would not be coming to an end anytime soon. I was never very patient, and the hospital stay was testing my patience more.

One day, when Mom and Dad were visiting, I asked, "Can I be tutored too? I know I can do it."

"We'll have to talk to the doctor about it," they said. I knew they would support whatever Dr. Jackson said. The next day, Dr. Jackson came in and said, "You'd like to be tutored, huh?"

"Yeah!"

"Randy," he said, pulling a chair up to the bed. "We're just afraid this would be too much for you with all the physical and occupational therapy you have to do."

My heart sank.

"I know therapy is very demanding," he said. "And being tutored could be more than you can handle. How about we see how things are going down the road a bit?"

I was intensely disappointed and disheartened. I knew I was capable of handling both therapy and school. School was just what I needed. I *wanted* to be tutored, but I also *needed* it more than anything.

Dr. Jackson wasn't being unreasonable. I was still only sitting up for a limited time, vomiting occasionally, my tracheotomy was still in place, and I wore the neck brace. However, there was something inside me that just knew I could handle being tutored. It was as if God was telling me to fight for this.

When Mom visited a few days later, I said, "Mom, I know I can manage going to school and doing therapy!"

"Randy, I'm sorry," she said, "but the doctor thinks it'll be too much for you."

"Please, let me at least try it," I begged. I was determined, unyielding.

"I'll mention it to Dr. Jackson one more time," she said.

"Thank you so much, Mom! Tell him I know I can do it."

Later that day, the doctor came in and said, "So you really want try being tutored, don't you?"

"Yes, I really do!"

"Let's try this," he said. "We'll give it a two week trial period, okay?"

"That would be great!" I replied.

"If we see it's going to be too much for you," he said, "we'll have to stop." He had a half smile on his face as he headed for the door. "I'll see you in the morning."

It was probably the longest conversation I ever had with Dr. Jackson. He was a kind man, but as a shy kid, I normally would never challenge an authority figure. I prayed in thanks to God for giving me the strength to stand up for what I knew I could do. I knew I'd have to work hard, but I was ready.

When Eric and I started tutoring, the days got much busier. We had to get our morning cares done, head down to PT, then OT, and back to First East for dinner. Our first tutoring sessions were in the early afternoon, followed by another PT session, another tutoring session at 4:00 p.m. and then back to First East for supper. Then, once a week, we had one more tutoring session at 7:00 p.m. Our tiny classroom was just off the waiting room for therapy. Many times we'd go to PT right after school. I was still spending most of my time on the cart, which made for a cramped room. We learned English, spelling, social studies, and history from Mrs. Fielding. She gave us weekly spelling tests and other tests. Mine were oral exams since I couldn't write.

She was the hospital tutor, and she was familiar with our daily routine. If I had to vomit, she'd help me. When I'd say, "Thank you," she'd reply, "Let me know if I can help you again." Mrs. Fielding was in touch with my school back home too. She kept tabs on what they were learning so I could be up to speed when I returned, making sure I'd be at the proper grade level.

Our math class was taught by Mr. Rankin, who came to tutor us once he was finished teaching at one of the Rochester junior high schools. He was a no-nonsense, "get right to the lesson" kind of guy. He taught us pre-algebra math. Unlike the hospital tutor, I never connected with him on a personal level. We met with him three times a week.

Science was taught by Miss Adams one night a week. A tiny lady, Miss Adams wore high heels, and we could always hear the click of her shoes announcing her pending presence. She taught us about reproduction. This was no big deal to me since I was familiar with the reproduction of animals, lessons from growing up on a farm. Bulls had to breed cows so calves could be born. Eric, however, wasn't familiar with reproduction at all. One night, he wanted me to explain it. Try to imagine two twelve-year-olds back in the 1960s having this discussion. I explained by talking about the farm animals.

"What about babies?" he asked.

How am I going to explain this? I wondered.

"A man and woman get married, and then they want to have kids, so they reproduce to have a baby," I tried.

He just couldn't understand.

The aides working that night got wind of our conversation and decided to have fun with it. One came into our room and asked, "What you guys talking about?"

"Nothing," we said, embarrassed.

A bit later, a different aide came in, pointed at my roommate, and asked me, "You teaching him anything?"

"No," I said, red faced.

The staff got a kick out of this.

Overall, I was fortunate that school came fairly easy for me. We had homework too. Every night, I'd have Mom write down the answers for me. Once in a while, she would help me with a question. If we really got stuck, Julie was always willing to help.

School passed the time in the hospital. It felt good to be mentally stimulated. My therapists in PT got my concentration level very high, and I left those sessions mentally and emotionally drained, but school was different. I was learning new things and loving it! The two week trial period quickly came to an end. I hoped that Dr. Jackson would evaluate everything and agree to let me continue. My grades were good, which I hoped would help. Above all, and I couldn't translate this to the doctor, I was feeling better emotionally and turning to God more for my needs.

When Dr. Jackson met with my parents, therapists, and tutors, I was nervous. I anxiously awaited the results. "Everyone is happy with your progress, so you can continue with school," Mom reported.

I was thrilled! My parents were smiling and shared in my excitement.

"We're proud of you, Randy!" said Dad. It's difficult for me to describe how good that made me feel. I never wanted to disappoint them and always wanted to make them proud.

Dr. Jackson stopped by later in the day. "You're doing a good job," he said. "Keep up the good work."

Having Dr. Jackson, a man of few words, stop to validate my hard work meant the world to me. All the effort my parents took to teach me my work ethic was paying off big time.

In many ways, I was fortunate to be tutored. You can hardly beat a 2:1 student to teacher ratio. We worked on so many subjects in those one hour sessions. The only downside was that when the teacher asked a question, there was a 50 percent chance I'd get called on to answer it. But, if I was prepared, I had nothing to worry about. As the saying goes, "Failing to prepare is preparing to fail." I could not rest or enjoy something if I had something that needed to be done. This applied to my homework too. Only if I got it done could I enjoy visiting with the other patients

Having Eric as my only classmate was also great. He excelled in social studies and history, and I did well in spelling and math. We fed off each other. Often, in the early morning, before the day shift came on duty, we'd have the night aide set us up for studying. My roommate could do most of this by himself, but I had an aide put the head of my bed up and the hospital table across my lap with my book stand on it, and get my book in place. Then, we studied. This created an even greater bond between us. We always cheered for each other.

As the first quarter of our education drew to an end, I knew I'd be getting a report card any day. I was anxious to see my grades. As it turned out, I was on the honor roll. I was proud of myself, and my parents were proud of me. My name was printed in the Austin, Minnesota, newspaper with other honor students. I got cards and letters from family, friends, and former teachers who were all proud of me. The hospital staff and fellow patients were also happy for me. They lifted my spirits more.

Tutoring classes were part of my life for many months to come. I was blessed to have great tutors in the hospital. They taught me many things and helped expand my mind. With my mind stimulated, it only made me want to learn more about what I was studying, but I also wanted to understand the growing peace and strength I felt coming from God when I prayed. The tutoring helped draw me closer to God than I ever had before. I prayed every night and shot arrow prayers to Him during the day. At first, I wasn't sure I had the right words when I prayed, but soon realized there are no right or wrong words. My body had been damaged physically, but I was growing spiritually and intellectually. These strengths would be much more beneficial to me throughout my life to come than a strong physical body.

CHAPTER 14
PHYSICAL AND OCCUPATIONAL THERAPY

"Whatever you do, work heartily, as for the Lord and not for men."
—Colossians 3:23

The most demanding thing I've ever done is go through physical therapy sessions. The sessions lasted forty-five minutes. The first five minutes were for small talk. Then, it was all business. What made it a bit easier was having two of the best physical therapists around, Allen and Gary, who were in their early twenties. They alternated between St. Marys Hospital and Mayo Clinic every six weeks, so when I didn't have one, I had the other. Working with them was comfortable. They became good friends. We talked about what was going on in each other's lives. Family was always a favorite topic. Gary was married, and Allen was engaged. We also talked about sports, the farm, and many other thoughts. It depended on what was happening in the world.

But we never talked long. PT was very important, and we had to get to work. Allen and Gary walked a fine line between being my drill sergeants and my friends. On one hand, they pushed me very hard. On the other, they knew when to hold back so as not to break my spirit by pushing me over the edge. They were great therapists and quality people. In fact, when I was able to sit up on a more routine basis, about six to eight months after my accident, Gary invited me over to his apartment for supper. It was late November of 1966, and I had gotten my first manual wheelchair. The back tires had air in them so I could be pushed around the farm terrain easier once I got home. It made transportation anywhere easier. So, Gary got permission from Dr. Jackson to take me to his apartment for supper.

"Are you ready to go?" he asked when he arrived.

"Sure am!" I said with enthusiasm. I was about to leave the hospital for only the second time since I'd arrived. I couldn't wait!

Gary lifted me into his car, put my wheelchair in the back seat, and drove to his home.

"Guess what we're having for supper," he asked on the way.

"Hamburger?"

"No, guess again."

"Pork chops?"

"No," he said. "One last guess."

"Meatloaf?"

"No."

"What is it?" I asked.

"Guess you'll just have to wait until we get there and be surprised," he said.

It wasn't long. Gary didn't live far from the hospital. When we arrived, he tilted my chair back on the rear tires and slowly wheeled me down, step by step, into their basement apartment. Instantly, I smelled the unmistakable scent of tomato sauce. "It's spaghetti!" I said.

"Finally! You guessed it!" he said.

It smelled remarkable. The scent took me back home to meals on the farm because we certainly never had food like that in the hospital. It felt great to get out and be in a homey atmosphere. I complimented Gary's wife on the meal.

"I'm happy to make it for you and glad you could come visit us," she said.

Gary did a good job feeding me that night. And that's no small task with spaghetti. That evening was another unforgettable act of kindness and caring. Those kindnesses made the transition to rigorous therapy easier. In fact, I even looked forward to going to therapy because of Allen and Gary, their friendship, and their "never give up" attitude, which I adopted.

In therapy, one of the first experiences I had was the tilt table. The therapist at the time, either Gary or Allen, transferred me from my cart to the table, strapping me down and cranking the head of the table up. The idea was to get me in as much of a standing position as possible. But I couldn't go very far before I got lightheaded and nauseous. The therapist knew my limitations and respected them. He'd check in at every stage to see how I was feeling. If I was starting to feel ill, he'd quickly crank the table flat.

Each day, I also had normal range stretching. This kept my muscles loose. I left those sessions mentally, physically, and emotionally exhausted. My therapists asked for and got my highest level of concentration as I concentrated on different muscle groups and memorized muscles in my arms and shoulders. The therapists wanted knowing these muscle groups to become second nature to me, and it did. I had everything from biceps to triceps to trapezoids and everything in between memorized. They'd quiz me on these muscles too. Then, I'd work incredibly hard on moving one muscle. Once, my therapist took out a wooden tray with powder on it and placed my hand and arm on it.

"Okay, Randy," he said. "Try pulling your hand toward your stomach."

I took a deep breath, closed my eyes, gritted my teeth, pictured my hand pulling toward my stomach, and tried as hard as I could.

It wouldn't move.

It's hard to describe the disappointment and confusion I felt when the muscles wouldn't respond. Before the accident, I could walk, run, jump, and throw a ball without even realizing my brain was telling my body what to do. Now, no matter how hard I tried and concentrated, I couldn't even move my little finger. Life changed in an instant. I had taken everything for granted before my accident. And now, when one shoulder moved a tiny bit, it was exhilarating. My hard work had been worth it! My therapists were encouraging yet relentless.

"You're moving your shoulder," they'd say. "What muscle do you need to use to do this?"

"Bicep."

"That's right," he said. "Now try again."

I repeated it with the same results.

"You're doing great. Try again."

After a few more tries, he'd say, "We need to stop now so you can get to OT. Randy, I'm very proud of you! You're a hard worker. We'll try it again this afternoon, okay?"

I felt exhausted on all levels. But it was on to OT. Here, I was blessed with a caring OT therapist named Laura. She was in her thirties and was my therapist throughout my entire hospital stay. From her, I learned how to use mouthsticks. This was very challenging and painstakingly slow. The first one they placed in my mouth seemed very heavy, but she still wanted me to hold it for a little while. "You'll get used to it," she said. One of the first things I did with it was use it to make a trivet. I had to move these yellow and brown ceramic tiles with my stick to make a design. Slowly, I moved the tiles to their appropriate places.

"Great job, Randy!" Laura would say, clapping. She recognized the seemingly smallest accomplishments. Making this trivet took me many thirty-minute sessions. Laura helped by placing glue around the tiles to keep them in place. It felt great when I was finished.

"What are you going to do with it?" asked Laura.

Without hesitation, and with a smile, I said, "Give it to Mom!"

"I'm sure she'll love it," said Laura.

Of course, Mom did. It was a good feeling to give her something. She had given so much to me and been with me through everything.

In OT, I also learned how to type on an old fashioned manual typewriter. I had to push really hard on those keys. It really helped build my neck muscles. Ironically, even though I broke my neck, my neck muscles and jaw became my strongest muscles. As time went on, I got better and better at typing. The first time I typed my name thrilled me. Over time, the mouthstick became second nature, but it certainly took getting used to it. The mouthsticks, in a way, are my arms and hands. Using them allowed me to be much more independent. Once I got my motorized wheelchair, I learned how to operate it in OT. Surprisingly, this didn't take long. But what freedom this allowed me! These successes were welcomed and much needed. Thanks to the encouragement and support of my therapists, I gained much needed skills that would help me maintain a fairly independent lifestyle. It also brought me another step closer to my goal of home.

CHAPTER 15
EVENINGS ON FIRST EAST

"He will yet fill your mouth with laughter,
and your lips with shouting."
—Job 8:21

Evenings were my favorite part of each day. After supper, most of us gathered in the hallway to visit. We didn't watch a lot of television. My aunt had given me a small black and white set to use once I got on First East. From time to time, I'd watch a show, but most of the time, we socialized. My roommate and I went to the nurse's station each evening to find out who our aide would be the next morning. We liked most of the aides, but had our favorites and were always excited if we were told it would be Jill or Nancy.

We also talked about the day's therapies, revisiting successes and setbacks. Often, we rejoiced over a fellow patient's new accomplishment. I remember the excitement we all felt when I got my motorized wheelchair in the winter of 1967. It was a big deal because no one else had one. The other quadriplegics, except the man in the iron lung, had enough arm movement to wheel their chairs by pushing the pegs that were attached to their chair rims. It didn't take me long to learn how to operate it with my mouthstick. And the freedom! It was such a blessing to gain more independence. I could go where I wanted to, for the most part. The aides loved to have fun, so it came as no surprise when Nancy presented me with a speeding ticket . Everyone got a good laugh out of that.

Nights also meant the occasional popcorn treat from the aides, who spent, with some of the nurses, their downtime with us. Some even asked us to go on break with them. Here was their opportunity to take a break and get away from us, yet they invited us along. And on First East, we had the freedom to go with them down to the basement break area near the vending machines. With its sterile white look and cement walls, it had a terrible, dark and dreary dungeon feel. There was talk of a morgue down the hall. It was eerily quiet. I didn't like the atmosphere but enjoyed being there while they had a snack and perhaps a cigarette. In those days, smoking was allowed in the hospital by staff, patients, and visitors. There were even ashtrays in the rooms. Sometimes the staff members would sneak in and have a cigarette when work slowed down. There was even one patient who smoked a cigarette through his tracheotomy. He wasn't from First East, but he couldn't move his limbs. His wife held the cigarette up to his tracheotomy, and he inhaled. I didn't give a second thought to anyone else smoking, but I was mystified by that sight.

When the aides were done with break, we went back to First East, which usually meant bedtime. Most patients needed assistance getting into bed and with their nightly cares. As usual, it took two aides to get me into bed in a two person lift. The male aide stood behind me, put his arms under my shoulders, reached down, and grabbed my wrists with his hands while the female aide grabbed under my legs. On the count of three, they lifted me up on my bed. The male aide did the bulk of the lifting, standing behind me. This procedure was simply reversed when they had to lift me out of bed. Imagine having someone, not family, put you in bed each night. Sometimes, it could be embarrassing, especially to a teen. As I was being transferred from my bed to my chair one day, the female aide was adjusting my feet and legs in the chair while the male aide got my bottom positioned properly and dropped my arms and hands into my lap. As my arms dropped, one of my fingers caught inside the neckline of the female aide's yellow uniform. She was bent over adjusting my feet, and when she bent back up, my finger was caught right inside her uniform neckline.

"Hey, what do you think you're doing?" she asked, teasing.

I wanted to crawl into a hole from embarrassment. My face turned every shade of red imaginable, and First East got quite a laugh at my expense. What's more, I didn't live it down for quite a while.

Another time, the aide assisting me was asked by a female aide to help lift someone else into bed. Bedtime was around nine. "I'll be right back," he promised. I never thought twice about it since this kind of thing happened all the time. My roommate was already sleeping, and I waited patiently. As time passed, I wondered what was taking him so long. More time passed. *This is taking way longer than it should*, I thought. Finally, I knew something was wrong because the 11:00 p.m. to 7:00 a.m. shift would soon be starting. I wondered if they forgot about me. I tried hollering to my roommate, but he was a heavy sleeper and there was no rousing him.

"Can anyone hear me?" I shouted.

My respiratory system has been affected with my paralysis. I have little projection in my voice at all. No one could've heard me unless they were standing outside my door. By this time, the shift change had taken place, and there were a limited number of staff members on duty. Over and over I shouted, with no response. I was scared and felt helpless. A sense of panic set in. I had to get off my bottom to prevent pressure sores. Even though I was strapped in, I could feel the weight more and more on my bottom. Finally, Julie, in the room next to me, heard me holler. *Thank God*, I thought.

"What's wrong?" she shouted. After I told her, she tried yelling for help too, but got no response. Then, she used the phone in her room to get the hospital operator and had her connect with the nurses' station. Next thing I knew, a couple staff members rushed in and transferred me into bed. I came to find out, the male aide who was assisting me before had hurt his back doing the other transfer and was down in the emergency room. They apologized over and over. Today, that sort of thing would never happen because there are different means of getting a nurse's attention. You can push the nurse's button with your mouth or head. They even have voice activated beds. But, looking back, this story makes me chuckle.

Of all the sights and sounds of First East, the one I recall the most is laughter. The kind and caring people there, with so many different personalities, became my second family as I spent eighteen months with them—more time during that period than I spent with my family. And each of us helped one another to learn and grow.

CHAPTER 16
LIFE LESSONS

"I can do all things through Christ
who strengthens me."
—Philippians 4:13

Although the vast majority of everyone I met at St. Marys was an angel during my stay, there were just a few who stand out in my memory for their unkindness.

Dr. Jeffrey Johnson, who was studying under Dr. Jackson, observed my physical therapy session on occasion. Years before, he had been in a car/train accident and lost both of his legs. It was inspirational because he got around well with two wooden legs and a cane. But, whether bitterness over his accident or just his own human nature, he was neither kind nor compassionate. Each time I heard the squeaky, wooden sound of him coming down the hall, I felt physically nauseated. He was always angry, and I never once saw him smile or joke around. Once, he was in my room examining me when his cane, which he had propped against the wall, fell to the floor. My dad bent down to pick it up.

"Leave it there! I can get it myself," he barked in an angry tone. Dad straightened and clearly didn't know what to think or say. He was only trying to help.

Another time, in PT, my therapist had me inclined as far as I could manage on the tilt table when Dr. Johnson decided I could be tilted farther.

"He can be tilted up more than that," he said.

"No," said my therapist. "That's as far as he can go without getting sick."

As the doctor went to crank the tilt, my therapist warned him again, yelling, "Stop!" But Dr. Johnson would not be deterred. Sure enough, as he cranked it higher, I grew quite ill, vomited, and nearly fainted.

My therapist was livid, quickly cranked the table back down, and had an attendant take me back to my room. Then, he marched down to see Dr. Jackson. After hearing what my therapist had to say, he immediately had Dr. Johnson removed from my case. This was a tremendous relief for me. I no longer had to worry when I heard his footsteps in the hall. I still saw him in the halls, but he never said a word to me.

The attitude of Ann Richards, the head nurse on the 11:00 p.m. to 7:00 a.m. shift, also had an impact. I can still remember her horn-rimmed glasses and her stoic, "I'm the boss" demeanor. She too never smiled or said anything kind. Each night, I always hoped the nurse's aide would come in to do my cares and not Nurse Richards. Since my body took a long time to adjust to my injury, I vomited quite a bit. When I did, it made a significant mess in my bed. Nurse Richards always got upset about cleaning me up. She even told me once in a grumpy voice, "Now don't make another mess!"

"I'm sorry, thanks," I said quietly. She never responded. I truly feared her presence. Sometimes, I'd even forego things I wanted done just to have her leave.

Nights were hard for me. When the nurses turned the lights out, tears rolled down my cheeks. I felt alone, and home seemed like another world away. I never cried very long, though. Since I couldn't wipe away the tears, I wanted to make sure they dried before a nurse returned. I prayed every night, "God, please let her be nice tonight." It wasn't just when she came on duty that I might see her. The overnight shift usually had one nurse and an aide on duty. We had to be turned from one side to the other every two hours to help prevent bed sores. I knew she'd be back in with the aide to turn me. I dreaded having her in my presence.

When a sympathetic aide said, "Don't worry about her. I'll come in and check on you," I felt immense relief.

Dad always told me to thank every hospital staff member for doing anything for me. "Without their help," he'd remind me, "you'd never get better." Of course, Dad was right. I always said thank you to everyone: therapists, doctors, nurses, aides, and even the catheter guys. It didn't matter how big or small the act was that they helped me with, I always said thank you when they finished. I said it from my heart too. But thanking this doctor and nurse was difficult. I did it, though my heart wasn't in it.

Over the years, I've grown in my ability to forgive and understand. Dr. Johnson and Nurse Richards were likely people going through troubles who were unhappy in their lives. As challenging as it was, I had to learn to forgive and even pray for their sufferings to ease rather than bearing a grudge. If there's one good thing that came from me knowing them, it was an increased appreciation for the rest of the hospital staff.

CHAPTER 17
HALLOWEEN

*"And He told them a parable to the effect
that they ought always to pray
and not lose heart."*
—Luke 18:1

The end of October marked five months in the hospital. Right after my accident, it had never occurred to me that I'd be there for five days, let alone five months. There was still a long road of therapy ahead, but my appetite was back and I had finally quit vomiting. This period was also when I met several significant milestones.

The first major milestone was getting the tracheotomy removed. Because the tracheotomy had been in place so long, everything seemed so different. I could breathe fine, but it was unusual feeling because I hadn't done it in so long. It was a huge relief, though, not having to worry about having it suctioned out or having the painful dressing changed. I adjusted quickly.

During this time, my neck brace was also removed for good. The brace supported my neck, which had been weakened because of my spinal cord injury. The adjustment to its removal took longer. Whereas before, I had been in my wheelchair, using my mouthsticks in OT, now, they limited the amount of time I could sit up. I no longer had support in my neck, and I certainly hadn't built up the necessary strength to support it on my own. The only way to strengthen my neck muscles was to gradually sit up for longer and longer periods of time. I wanted to push myself as far as I could, but there was a fine line between strengthening my neck muscles and overdoing it. My therapists made sure I went at a steady pace.

During this period, I had a lot of time to ponder. I wondered how things were going back home. I was sure the second crop of hay was in the loft, and the soybeans were harvested. Dad had probably chopped some corn and put it in the silo as feed for the cows. He'd probably picked some corn. Sometimes we were still harvesting corn at Thanksgiving. It all depended on the weather. The usual chores like milking cows, bedding the animals, feeding, cleaning out the barn and other buildings, and everything else had to be done, along with harvesting the crops. Fall was busy on the farm, and Dad worked long days harvesting the crops. I missed helping out. I was certain Jim was busy too, and I was a bit jealous that he got to do so many of the things I loved with Dad. Above all, I kept thinking about deer hunting. To go deer hunting, you had to be twelve and have a firearm safety certificate. I'd just gotten my certificate two weeks before my accident, and was anxious to deer hunt with Dad, Jim, my uncles, and some older cousins. The deer hunting stories they all shared captivated me. I wanted to be part of it, but it wasn't meant to be. It wasn't hard to feel disappointed and blue about this loss. I didn't want to feel that way, so I prayed.

To return a bit of cheer to the air and not get mired in self-pity, I turned to something I had always enjoyed: Halloween. Eric and I had a plan. We were certain Halloween was a day to be celebrated even in a hospital. It was a time of excitement and diversion. Between us, we decided there shouldn't be school on Halloween, so we started a petition for no school that day. We got an unbelievable number of people to sign it. It was over two pages long. We counted just over a hundred names. Our fellow patients were happy to sign it, most aides and nurses, attendants, orderlies, catheter guys, therapists, and even some doctors, too. There were some impressive names on that petition, people with power. Our tutor didn't stand a chance. She gave in and let us have Halloween off.

We held a party with the help of my mom and Eric's mom. They got permission from the head nurse, a very businesslike nun, Sister Margaret. Although nice, Sister Margaret laughed very little. It was a surprise that she got so involved with this party. She even helped with the planning. Everyone was invited to join us in the dining room to celebrate. Many staff members came even though they were off duty. My therapists came and helped transfer me from the cart to my chair. I wasn't able to sit up long yet since I had just gotten my neck brace removed. They transferred me back to the cart after being up for a short time, and I was able to enjoy the rest of the party from there.

Many people dressed up in costume. Mom came as a jailbird. She wore a striped outfit and had a ball and chain. I dressed up as a Native American. Mom made me an outfit from a gunny sack. I even wore a headband with a feather. Some of the nurses and aides dressed up too. There were people dressed in costumes that ranged from ghosts and witches to scarecrows and other popular characters. The party featured sandwiches, salads, punch, and goodies. I remember eating a Nut Goodie candy bar. It was quite the treat since I hadn't had much candy in a long while. The highlight of the party was this game Mom and Eric's mother had developed. Many people today are familiar with it, but it was a relatively new experience then. People had to reach in through different holes in boxes and guess what they were feeling. For instance, peeled grapes were eyeballs, large noodles were intestines, and mushy melons were brains. I couldn't reach in to feel the things but had a great time watching others try. Most of the First East patients had turned out to celebrate, from the oldest patients to my roommate and me. But, above all, it was a break from routine and a day filled with much needed laughter.

The best part? My brothers and sisters came. At this point, I hadn't seen them since the county fair in early August. Since they technically weren't allowed because they were too young, the staff turned their heads and pretended my siblings weren't there. The staff knew this meant the world to me. It was the best medicine available.

Randy Krulish

As time went on, I was able to sit up longer and return to the hard work of OT and PT. It was probably mid to late November before I was able to accomplish this. This party did a lot to lift my spirits and give me the strength I needed to dedicate to the hard work ahead.

CHAPTER 18
FIRST EXPERIENCES

*"Finally, all of you, have unity of
mind, sympathy, brotherly love,
a tender heart, and a humble mind."*
—1 Peter 3:8

In some ways, I was a naïve kid when I broke my neck. I hadn't lived a sheltered life, but it had been simple and uncomplicated. While I was aware of the facts of nature, I was unaware of many ways of the world. A lengthy stay in the hospital opened my eyes to some new ideas and issues.

In my twelve years, I had never known anyone or known of anyone who had gone through a divorce. None of my family members, classmates, or friends had ever experienced this. I knew what divorce was, but that was the extent of my knowledge. The hospital was full of broken relationships. Remember Tom, the man who always had a Bible on his lap? His wife had left him after his accident. But I saw other broken relationships too. One in particular hit close to home. Eric's parents were going through a divorce. This was hard on him and very painful. We never really talked about it, but my heart ached for him. Eric was withdrawn—not his usual cheery self. Our moms had become good friends. His mom had a very infectious laugh. Hearing it always made me smile. His dad was a quieter man, but still friendly. I wondered how it would feel to have my parents divorce. I thought it would feel as if I were being torn apart—part of me would go with one parent and part with the other. Though I'd been praying a lot by this time, I began to realize the need to pray more for others. I was growing in compassion, and my eyes were opening wider to the sufferings of others. God taught me more compassion through the pain my roommate was experiencing.

In addition to divorce, I had never experienced any issues with sexual preference until I met Jennifer, a fellow patient on First East. She had light brown hair and was twenty-five-years-old. A car accident resulted in her becoming a paraplegic. Jennifer was a kind, fun, and light-hearted patient who was a perfect fit for the First East family. She soon became friends with us all. I really enjoyed being around her. Mom got to know her as well. A lot of the female patients would confide in Mom. She is very tenderhearted. As with your own family, the patients and visitors on First East often went into one another's rooms and visited. One day, Mom was going into Jennifer's room to visit and got the shock of her life. The door was open, so Mom knocked on the door frame and called her name. When she got no response, she called her name a few more times before walking in a bit farther. To her surprise, she saw Jennifer in bed with a female staff member. Mom left quickly and felt quite embarrassed. When Mom returned to my room, I could tell that something had happened, but I had no idea what. Jennifer came by shortly after and, very simply, explained to Mom that she was gay. Mom apologized for walking in on her, but Jennifer told Mom it wasn't her fault.

Though I was present, I still had no idea what was happening. Some of the other patients were aware of Jennifer's situation and had been talking about it too. What did it all mean? Finally, I asked Mom, "What's going on?"

"You know how when you get older, you will date girls and maybe someday marry a woman?" she asked.

"Yeah."

"Jennifer would rather date another woman instead of a man," said Mom, matter-of-factly.

I must have looked as confused as I felt.

"Jennifer is called a lesbian. Sometimes people who like other people of the same sex are called gay," said Mom.

I still wasn't sure what Mom was talking about. What did this mean for our friendship? "Will she be different now?" I asked.

"She'll be the same person you've always known," said Mom.

And that was good enough for me. I had never heard the word *homosexual*. I thought gay was another word for happy. But, as the days went by, I found out Mom was right. In the interchange I had with Jennifer and other patients, everyone seemed the same. We all just carried on with our lives as usual. I realized then and there that there are many things in life I don't understand, but it's not my job to judge either.

Loss was another topic I had learned about and had to come to terms with on First East. Eric had completed his therapy and was headed home, which meant that I would get a new roommate. Brian, who was from Rochester, was eighteen-years-old. He'd been a lifeguard and had big strong arms and shoulders. His story was just as tragic as that of others on First East. Brian had tingling and numbness in his legs, so he went to the doctor to have it checked out. They couldn't find anything wrong with him, and things kept getting worse. He went to several more doctors, but none found anything wrong. Eventually, his legs were completely paralyzed. The doctors found no physical reason for his paralysis, so they sent him to the psychiatric ward, thinking it was psychological. Eventually, they decided to do one last test, and it was here that they found a large malignant tumor pressing on his spinal cord. By the time they found it, there was nothing they could do because the tumor was inoperable. This was when he was moved to First East, where he became my roommate. When I heard his story, it all seemed so senseless. I couldn't understand it.

Mom, Dad, and I became good friends with him and his parents. His Dad owned a store in Rochester. When he found out I enjoyed sports, he gave me an autographed picture of the Minnesota Twins baseball team. I loved it! Mom took it home and framed it. Dad wasn't at the hospital every day anymore, but when he was, he talked sports with Brian, who'd been involved in high school sports. It was an interest we all shared.

Brian was always pleasant and had a good attitude. He never complained about his situation. I was inspired by his love of life and his will to just live. During one visit, his mother said, "I wish they'd found this tumor sooner."

Brian refused to wallow in self-pity. He simply replied, "Mom, just be thankful my mind is okay." In a strange way, he was almost happy they found the tumor. He now knew there was a reason for his paralysis. It wasn't all in his head. He never talked about the effects the tumor would have on his life. He knew, as we all did, that he would die. He never showed fear or talked about it. I always wondered what he was thinking, if he felt any fear.

Once, when he wasn't in the room, Mom and I talked about his situation. She felt terrible for him. "Randy, Brian's pretty sick," she said.

"Do you think he'll get better?" I asked, knowing the answer already.

"I'm afraid he won't," she said. "The doctors can't help him anymore."

"Do you think he'll die?" I asked.

"He's very sick," she said, "but when he goes to heaven, he won't have any more pain."

I didn't respond. I couldn't. I didn't know what to say. But I took comfort in thinking he would one day no longer be in pain.

Brian's mom had a lot of anger. She was furious with the doctors for not finding the tumor sooner. Mom was a sounding board and a comfort for her.

I prayed a lot for Brian. "God, please make him better. Take away his pain and suffering." Soon, it got to the point where I only prayed for his pain to go away. I knew he was going to die.

As the days and weeks went by, you could see Brian slowly get weaker and weaker. It was hard watching this young man's strong body slowly deteriorate. He tried not to show it, but he was in pain. When he couldn't hold it in any longer, he moaned. I hated hearing it. It took me back many months to the sounds my ICU roommate made in pain. Brian couldn't talk much anymore either. His voice was weak, and his breathing had labored. Eventually, they moved him to a private room on First East. He was put on oxygen, so he could no longer have visitors. I continued to pray to God to take away his pain. It bothered me to know he was hurting. I knew he would die, I just didn't know how to handle it. Prayer gave me a certain peace about Brian's situation. Somehow, I knew God was with him.

Death was foreign to me. All of my grandparents were still alive, no friends had ever died, and I had never lost a family member. I began to think about it more. One night, I was partially awake when the night aide came in to turn me. I'd been wondering how Brian was doing, so I asked. She hesitated, finally answering, "Brian passed away about fifteen minutes ago."

I felt empty inside. It was my first death experience. It took me a while before I could fully focus on therapy again. My therapists understood. Julie made arrangements with the staff so we patients could attend Brian's funeral. It worked out well since the funeral was in Rochester. Many of the First East staff and patients attended. I never saw his parents after the funeral. Eventually, we lost touch with them.

All those months in the hospital made me see an entirely different world from the simple farm life I loved so much. I had always been a sensitive kid, but now I was able to see the pain and suffering others were going through. After all I had witnessed, I made the choice to put others first in my life. My daily prayers were always for my family and others before myself. I knew if others weren't hurting or struggling, then I felt better too!

CHAPTER 19
CHRISTMAS

"Jesus said, 'Give, and it will be given to you. A good measure, pressed down, shaken together, and running over, will be poured into your lap. For with the measure you use, it will be measured to you."
—Luke 6:38

As the holidays approached, I'd been in the hospital for seven months. By this time, according to the doctors, I had all of the movement and sensation I would ever likely regain following the accident. Over the past months, I'd gained touch, or surface, feeling throughout my body, and I could shrug my shoulders a bit. Considering my condition right after my accident, I'd come a long way. The tongs were gone. The tracheotomy was removed. I no longer wore a neck brace. I could talk on my own, use mouthsticks, operate my motorized wheelchair, and sit up for long periods of time. I'd become quite independent considering my level of quadriplegia. With that independence came a renewed sense of freedom.

Still, there remained troubling thoughts. I worried that I wasn't working hard enough—that I still had movement to gain back. Dad used to emphasize the importance of therapy and reinforce that I needed to work hard there, especially in PT. He knew PT was where I could gain movement back. I wanted to work hard for myself, but also to please him in those grueling PT sessions. But I never felt like I was doing enough. One day, I asked Mom, "Does Dad think I'm working hard in therapy?"

"Randy," my Mom said, "he thinks you're working very hard, and he's proud of you!" She could sense the emotion and meaning behind my words, so she explained further. "He always thought you'd get all of your movement back. It's somewhat hard for him to accept that you have to live the rest of your life in a wheelchair."

I was glad he was proud of me. And I realized this was the first talk I'd ever had with anyone about living my life from a wheelchair. Prior to this, it was something I just assumed. Now, it had been said out loud. I accepted it, and I never asked Mom about it again. It was difficult for Dad to have to come to terms with my paralysis. Like all parents, he wanted what was best for me. Mom and Dad knew my having to live life from a wheelchair would be a difficult challenge. But they were loving and supportive regardless! I clung to that like a lifeline, and returned their love by doing everything I could to be my best.

Sometimes, late at night, though, I'd give in to wondering what it was going to be like to never walk again. Emotionally, it overwhelmed me. I didn't like thinking about it, yet I couldn't quite escape it when I was alone at night. During the day, it didn't enter my mind much because I was busy with routine and surrounded by the positive attitudes of fellow patients. At night, however, it was quiet. I had more time to think once the lights went out. On occasion, I just felt tired of being in the hospital, and the tears would come. Prayers were my life support. "God, help me get through this," I'd ask. "I just want to go home." I developed a mantra that I repeated over and over to console myself: "When I get home, everything will be fine. When I get home, everything will be fine."

I turned thirteen one week before Christmas. Mom brought cards my siblings had made. Jill made me a birthday cake, and all of First East sang "Happy Birthday." My parents gave me a troll doll. It was a foot tall and donned a caveman outfit with long black hair. I loved it and kept it in my room for my entire hospital stay.

The approach of Christmas gave me an opportunity for distraction. Mom always made the holidays special at home. My siblings and I helped decorate Christmas cookies and the tree, hang lights, and spray white foam over outlines on the windows to make images of reindeer, Christmas trees, and more. My favorite Christmas gift, as a child, had been a green John Deere tractor that I pedaled up and down our sidewalk and driveway. This year, Mom worked hard to again make Christmas special even though I was spending it on First East. I was excited to hear my siblings would be joining us at St. Marys so we could celebrate together. It was a wonderful feeling to be close to my family again. Mom had decorated my room in holiday décor and made a number of traditional Christmas treats. Together, we sang my favorite hymn, "Silent Night." It filled me with a feeling of peace. Some of the other patients got to go home for a few days over Christmas, because they had improved enough through their recovery process. I wish it could've been me, but my family brought Christmas to me, and I loved it! I had the gift of family that day. Having them around was uplifting and truly the best gift I ever received.

But it wasn't the only gift I received. Joe was a patient on First East who was quiet and kept to himself. He was a hemiplegic, paralyzed on one side from a stroke. Joe never sat in the halls socializing and mingling with the rest of us. Some of the aides thought he was grumpy. Frequently, I saw him in OT. He was always working on a big, wooden machine that looked like a quilting machine. He was dedicated to it and worked diligently day after day. But he always took the time to say hi to me. I responded in kind, but it went no further than that. Joe was a mystery. After my family left for home that Christmas day, an aide brought in a large gift for me. Since I couldn't move my arms, she opened it. That gift was a cushion that could fit precisely between the arms of my chair, giving my hands a resting place. It was from Joe. His occupational therapist had gotten the exact measurements from my therapist so it would fit perfectly in my chair. It had a blue covering with multiple other colors woven into it. It was an amazing gift. I didn't know what to think. All I could do was ask the aide to tell him thanks and that I thought it was a wonderful gift. I used that cushion for months to come, until it finally wore out. I couldn't help think about the many times I saw him working hard in OT. All that time, he was making a gift for me. That night, I couldn't sleep very well thinking about my family, but most of all, about this wonderful gift from the mystery man. It touched my heart in a way no gift ever had. Tears of joy rolled down my cheeks.

The other patients were equally surprised he gave me a gift. Joe's therapist later told me Joe wanted to make a Christmas gift for me because he felt bad for me. "He had to work very hard to get it done by Christmas," she said. When I next saw Joe in OT, I was able to tell him thank you myself. "Does it work okay?" he asked. I assured him it did and was rewarded with a half smile, the closest I'd ever seen him come to a full smile.

We only ever exchanged pleasantries, even after that day, but I'd learned a wonderful lesson that Christmas: you never know what's in other peoples' hearts.

CHAPTER 20
WINTER ON FIRST EAST

"The Lord is good, a refuge in times of trouble.
He cares for those who trust in Him."
—Nahum 1:7

As the winter of 1967 wore on, the limited daylight hours passed by quickly. Sometimes, in the evenings, some of us patients would go up to the sixth floor and look out the window over the city of Rochester. Lights twinkled as far as I could see. It was a far cry from life on the farm. I'd been in the hospital about eight and a half months, and there had been some changes in my life. Mom had returned to working at the Hormel meat packing plant in Austin. This eased the family finances, since she'd been on an unpaid leave since my accident. This affected me a great deal as I saw her less. Visiting hours started at 11:00 a.m. every day. I used to listen for Mom's footsteps coming down the hall. She always stayed until close to suppertime. I never felt anxious when she was with me. Once she went back to work, she'd run over to see me as soon as work was over. This was mid-afternoon. She'd write down the answers to my homework assignments and leave again close to suppertime. It always felt empty when she left. But Mom needed to get home to see the rest of the family. I have no idea how she managed her job, me, and the farm. The time we spent together in the hospital was our time to bond. Our special connection started there and grew. She became not just my mother, but also one of my best friends.

With Mom not being around as much, I focused my energies even more on school. It provided an escape from the daily routine on First East. I was fortunate to maintain good grades. I worked hard in therapy too. But during this time, I began to plateau. There was no longer any noticeable improvement in my muscles. Everything was at a standstill. My therapists continued to have me work hard, but nothing was changing. Although this bothered me, I continued working hard.

Weekends seemed as long as winter to me. I never liked weekends on First East. There was no routine, and the days never ended. Monday through Friday, we had a schedule to follow. I'm a very scheduled person and like to follow routine, but scheduled was the last thing weekends were. We received our meals at the usual times, but that was the only similarity to weekdays. Our morning cares were handled when the aides weren't busy with someone else. Then, we'd wait for dinner. After dinner, there wasn't much to do. It was the longest part of the day. Many of the other patients had progressed far enough in therapy to go home for the weekend. I was jealous, but I knew if I worked hard, my time would come.

The one good thing about weekends was that I'd sometimes get visitors, such as aunts and uncles. Of course, Mom and Dad would be there for part of the day too. I always looked forward to mid-afternoon on Saturdays because mail would be delivered. I was always excited to see if I got anything. By now, the mail I received had slowed down considerably. Some days, I didn't get anything. It was always disheartening. I wondered what my friends were doing back home. I didn't feel forgotten about, but I realized life went on for everyone. My broken neck now seemed secondary to life in general. After my accident, there was so much focus on my situation. Now I felt alone more. I was suppressing feelings of darkness. I tried not to show this because everyone wanted me to be strong. I was smiling on the outside, but crying inside. It hurt keeping this pain inside. To me, showing it meant showing weakness. I'm not sure why I never let others into my perceived world of darkness. That winter, I learned I was human and pain is a part of life. Weekends that winter meant I had more time to think about things like this. I liked alone time to pray and thank God for His many blessings, but I had to be careful about too much alone time. It gave me too much time to think about the bad things in life.

But the winter of 1967 taught me something important. It helped me see my accident differently. I was no longer the center of attention. I realized that I loved it that way. I was never one to enjoy the spotlight, preferring the background instead. On First East, we were all on a level playing field. Each patient had a life-changing accident and was working hard in therapy. With so much time on my hands, I learned patience. I learned to be happy for my fellow patients who went home on weekends, not jealous. I also realized my time there would not be forever. I knew that soon I'd be going home on weekends also. Just as winter turned to spring, surely there was light ahead of the darkness.

CHAPTER 21
SPRING BRINGS CHANGE

*"And after he had taken leave of them,
he went up on the mountain to pray."*
—Mark 6:46

Near the first part of March, a few of the faces on First East had changed. Some fellow patients had gone home for good, and there had been a small turnover in staff members. This happened gradually, so I didn't notice it too much. What I did notice, though, was when Julie went home. It was hard to see her leave. Even though I was happy for her, her departure left a huge hole in First East. And it was hard for her to say good-bye too. She personally went from room to room saying good-byes. By the time she got to my room, her face was red with emotion and tears were streaming down her cheeks. I admired her very much. I used to imagine that when I grew up and had a family of my own, that I would want to name my daughter after her. That's the kind of impact she had on my life. When she stopped in my room, Mom gave her a bracelet she had bought as a good-bye gift from us. Julie cried even more when she opened it.

"Randy," she said, "you are a fine young man, and I know you'll be successful at whatever you do. I'll miss you and your mom so much. You are like family to me."

She too had a gift for me. "You can open it after I leave," she said. "I love you. Good-bye!" She then wheeled out my room. I was sad watching her leave.

"Do you want to open her gift?" Mom asked. I did. Julie had given Mom a big blue absorbent pad that we all called chux. It's a pad they placed on our beds over the sheets to absorb any urine that leaked from our catheters or incontinence. It protected our skin. The other side of the chux was a white cotton-like material. On the top half, she had written in red lipstick, "Randy, I wanted to give you something special! Something you'll never forget! Hope you enjoy it!" Then, Mom unfolded the bottom part. There was a lipstick kiss. I guess you could say Julie gave me my first kiss! I was a bit embarrassed with Mom there, but secretly enjoyed it. My friendship with Julie was strong. She taught me lessons in determination, laughter, kindness, and goodness. She was a strong lady who let nothing stop her. But Julie's leaving the hospital could not stop our friendship. Over the years, we stayed in touch, and I was even present at her wedding.

I missed Julie, but life moved on, and I was determined to keep working hard. So I was surprised, therefore, when Dr. Jackson came into my room one Tuesday that spring and asked, "How would you like to go home this weekend?" I was caught off guard, and maybe even hesitated a minute before responding, but couldn't contain my excitement when I said, "That would be great!"

"I need to talk to your parents about a couple things," he said. "Then you should be able to go home Friday afternoon when you're finished with afternoon PT." He gave a little smile at my obvious pleasure and left. When he was gone, I cried. But they were tears of joy. I prayed in thanksgiving. I hadn't been home in nearly ten months. Here I was, only three days away from returning. My mind was spinning. I almost didn't know how to feel. This had been my single goal for so long. And it was here. All I could think was to continue praising and thanking God. I never would've made it this far without His strength and love for me. He had been my lifeline in here.

When Mom came that afternoon, she had a huge smile on her face.

"I get to go home this weekend!" I said.

"I know!" she said. "I just have to meet with a couple nurses to go over your cares, and then your dad will pick you up Friday afternoon."

"I can't wait, Mom!"

"I can't either, because then we'll be together as a family again," she said.

It was just a formality that Mom had to meet with the nurses. She knew my cares better than anyone. As a matter of fact, many hospital staff members thought she had a medical background, because she picked up on my cares so quickly. I felt more comfortable having her and Dad handle my cares than anyone.

Soon, everything was arranged so I didn't have school on Friday afternoons, and my second PT session that day was scheduled for early afternoon. I'd be ready to go home for the weekend around 2:00 p.m. every Friday. The anticipation was acute. I knew everything I had endured over the past ten months, all of the therapy and hard work, had only made me stronger. I could now face the world knowing I was stronger and that I wasn't alone. I had a wonderful family, and God was always with me!

Chapter 22
Home

*"So that by God's will I may
come to you with joy
and be refreshed in your company."*
—Romans 15:32

When the day of my first trip home finally arrived, I went through the day's routine and returned to my room to find Dad waiting for me. He asked, with a huge grin on his face, "Are you ready to go home?"

"Sure am!" I replied.

There were few things I needed to take home since my parents had already gotten what they needed to do my cares. All the nurses, aides, therapists, and staff were happy for me. They knew this was a huge step toward going home for good. An aide walked with us down to the parking lot. Dad picked me up out of my chair and lifted me into the car. Once I was situated, we were headed home!

Joy is the perfect word to sum up what I was feeling. I didn't even care how long it took to get home. Just knowing we were headed there was enough. I was excited to see the farm and be with my family. Dad asked how PT went that day. We exchanged small talk about my siblings, neighbors, and other things happening around the farm on our way home. When Dad turned down our long dirt driveway, I could hardly contain my excitement. At the house, my whole family was there to greet me. Mom had just gotten home from work. I was amazed at how much my siblings had grown, but they still looked the same. Jim was now sixteen and a sophomore in school, Becky was eleven and in fifth grade, Bob was seven and in first grade, and Linda was still three and not in school yet. She had a babysitter when Dad was busy with farm work. Dad got me out of the car and placed me in my wheelchair. The first thing I noticed was how the air felt very cool, but smelled so clean and fresh—country fresh. Mom made the adjustments on my chair to make me comfortable. We didn't have a ramp yet, so Dad tilted me back on my rear tires and pulled me up the steps, one by one. My siblings were anxious to help in any way they could. When we got inside the house, we were in the dining room. The first thing I noticed was some of the furniture had been moved. Then, I saw an old hospital bed in the corner. My uncle had gotten it at the VFW club, Veterans of Foreign War. The corner of the living room would be my room. Since I couldn't do stairs, I wouldn't be able to sleep in my bedroom upstairs that I had shared with Jim. This was a perfect solution. It was the biggest room in our house. The oil furnace was in this room, which made it even better since I now got colder easier.

Mom and Dad took turns sleeping on the living room couch. This way, they could easily hear if I needed help during the night. Sometimes, I'd have spasms that would kick my legs out of a comfortable position. They'd need to be readjusted. I'd also need to be turned during the night.

But I wasn't restricted to the dining room. I could easily get into the kitchen and living room, as the dining room was in the middle. For an old farmhouse, the building was quite accessible. And it was a comfort. Everything looked and smelled the same.

"Are you glad to be home?" Jim asked.

"Yeah, it's great!" I answered. Then, I just listened and watched. I enjoyed every moment I could with them. We all just kind of picked up from where we left off ten months ago. Becky was telling me about things she was doing in school. Linda wanted to crawl up on my chair. Pointing to my mouthstick, she asked, "What's this?"

"I'll show you in a little bit, okay?" I said. I wanted to see the rest of the house first. My mind was racing and it was hard to believe I'd been home for only a few minutes. Bob was his usual quiet self. With a smile, he asked, "Do you need help with anything?"

I answered, "Not right now, but thanks."

The kitchen was my favorite room in the house. It always smelled like Mom's cooking, the fragrance of flowers on the table, or craft smells from Mom's latest project. I loved eating our meals sitting around the kitchen table as a family—just the seven of us enjoying Mom's great cooking and talking about the daily activities. On my first day home, the kitchen smelled like beef pot roast, which was cooking in the oven with potatoes and carrots. It was going to be a tasty supper. Mom made the best gravy too. She served dinner with a fruit salad with oranges and bananas. We all enjoyed eating together. It was a typical farm meal with meat and potatoes, and quite a treat for me after eating hospital food for so long. Later that weekend, Mom made meatloaf and baked potatoes. This was, and still is, my favorite meal. While eating it, Mom fed me, but Linda quickly asked, "Can I feed him?"

Mom answered, "Sure, feed him a bite."

Linda took the fork, stuck it in a piece of potato, and placed it in my mouth. I bit down, and she pulled the fork out.

"Good job!" said Mom.

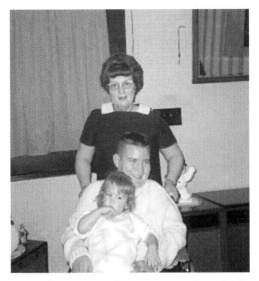

Mom, Linda, & me – home on weekends! (1967)

Linda had a big smile on her face. I swallowed and said, "Yeah, great job! Thanks, Linda!" She was so proud of herself. From then on, all my family members fed me whenever I needed their help. I never had to ask. Later that evening, I showed my siblings all the things I could do with my mouthstick. They were impressed.

The daily routine continued as I remembered it. Since it was still March in Minnesota, I didn't venture outside. I was reminded of the simplicity of farm life. It seemed so far removed from the complex world I had grown to know on First East.

At night, Jim helped Dad get me into bed, and then Mom did most of my cares with Dad helping. None of my cares were ever hidden from my siblings. If Mom was in the middle of bowel care, and they walked in, she'd just explain what she was doing. They all knew my cares were part of who I am.

The weekend went by fast, and I was disheartened when it was time to go back to First East on late Sunday afternoon. My family said good-bye. It hurt to leave them, but I knew I'd be back the next weekend. It was a quiet ride back to St. Marys Hospital that Sunday. It was starting to get dark by the time Dad and I returned. Dad told me he'd have a ramp ready for me by next weekend. When the aides were transferring me into bed, they asked how my weekend went. It was fun reliving it with them.

Weekends home were now part of the normal routine, and would be until I was released from the hospital. One Friday, however, when Dad came to get me, the head nurse told Dad, "Randy won't be able to go home this weekend." The nurse was older and very set in her ways. She never smiled much. She was a good nurse, but certainly not my favorite. My heart sank after hearing her. I felt sick thinking I'd spend the weekend in the hospital.

Dad asked why, and the nurse told him I'd developed a slight fever, and that hospital policy wouldn't let me be released until it was normal.

"I'll be right back," said Dad. I didn't know where he went. After a while Dad came back and said, "I talked to your doctor, and he said you can go home."

I was so happy, my spirits took flight again. Dr. Jackson had called the nurse and told her, "The best therapy Randy can have right now is to go home, so I'm authorizing it." This nurse wasn't happy Dad went over her head, but I knew Dad and my doctor did what was best for me. And they cared.

I was so thankful to be going home then and always. Those weekend visits home changed my entire view on life. On one hand, my heart ached for the patients who had to stay when I went home. I had been in their shoes, and I felt badly for them. But I had worked hard to reach this point. I learned to be thankful for every single blessing I had.

CHAPTER 23
HOME FOR GOOD

"But rejoice insofar as you share Christ's
sufferings, that you may also rejoice and
be glad when his glory is revealed."
—1 Peter 4:13

By the end of April, I had been going home on weekends for about six weeks and loving every minute. I was still concerned that PT had come to a standstill. I hadn't seen any improvements for several weeks. Eleven months had passed, and I was focusing on therapy, school, and weekends home. It wasn't long until my doctor asked to meet with my parents. This didn't concern me because he did so from time to time. After the meeting, all three came into my room. Now, I did begin to wonder because this had never happened before.

"Randy," said Dr. Jackson, "we think you're ready to go home to stay. How do feel about this?"

I couldn't believe what I was hearing! I was overwhelmed with joy! Could it be happening?

I could barely speak.

"Yeah," I said finally. "I think I'm ready!"

In hindsight, Dr. Jackson's question was silly, almost rhetorical. Maybe he just wanted to see and hear my reaction. What I remember the most is smiles from each of us.

"I know your parents can do your cares," said Dr. Jackson, "I just need to set things up for your schooling, and then you should be ready to go home on Friday. I'll talk to you later." And he left.

"I can't believe it! I'm going home," I shouted.

"What great news, huh?" said Mom. "We'll all be together as a family again." It was always about family to Mom.

"We'll all need to thank everyone we've met during your hospital stay," said Dad. I assured him I would. Gratitude was important to Dad.

I felt at peace. I had been through so much the past eleven months, and now it was just about over. It was almost more than I could comprehend. The hospital staff that had been part of my daily life for months no longer would be. While I felt wonderful about achieving my goal, it was tinged with sadness knowing I would be leaving fellow patients. It was hard for me to disconnect from this huge part of my life.

On Thursday, my favorite aide, Jill, was working. "I hear you're going home tomorrow," she said.

"Yeah, I'm excited!" Then, I told her she was my favorite aide, and I thanked her for her help.

"Randy," she replied, "I always hoped I'd get you as a patient. You're the nicest young man I've ever met."

I started to cry, and she cried with me. Then, she said, "If I give you my address, will you promise to write me?"

I promised. She wrote her address down and left it on my tray table. Then, she gave me a hug. I cried even more as she walked out of my room. Mom put her address with other addresses we'd collected.

Saying good-byes was hard. How do you turn off a switch and forget the people you cared for so much? I realized you couldn't, but I didn't know how to get through this emotionally. These one time strangers had become my hospital family. They had become angels sent to me by God to help me through this time of difficulty.

The only way I could get through the good-byes was by thinking about being home with my family. This brought the excitement back. On Thursday, the doctor came by.

"I talked with your teachers and school back home, and they all agreed since you're doing so well with your grades that it wouldn't be necessary for you to have tutors for just a month at home," he said.

"You mean I'm done with school this year?" I asked.

"Yes, you are, and you'll be ready for eighth grade in the fall," he said. "I'll see you in the morning before you leave," he added.

As he left, I knew I'd miss Dr. Jackson too. He was a quiet man with a big heart, and he cared deeply about his patients.

My last trip down to therapy was very hard too. I thanked Laura for all of her help in OT. She wished me the best, and we exchanged addresses. It was even harder saying good-bye to Gary, my physical therapist. "We've been through a lot, huh?" I agreed.

"You always worked so hard. I'll miss you," he said.

"I'll miss you too," I said as I began to cry.

"Everything will be okay, Randy," he said as he put his hand on my shoulder. "Now you'll be home with your family."

When my parents came, they said good-bye to our hospital family too. Among us, lots of hugs, addresses, and tears were exchanged. There wasn't much to transport since Mom had taken stuff gradually throughout the week. As we left, an aide walked down with us. After I was in the car, she said, "Good-bye, Randy! I'll miss you."

I replied, "Good-bye, I'll miss you too!" And I was on my way home!

On the drive, I reflected on the people I had met on my journey and how they had touched my life. I wondered if I would ever see them again. Over the years, I stayed in touch with many of them. But back then, all I knew was that I'd miss the nightly gatherings out in the hall. We shared our daily activities in those halls. It was mostly laughter and joys, but we shared pain and heartaches as well. So many emotions lingered in those halls. I'd also miss going with the aides on their breaks. I started to cry as we drove home. "Are you okay?" Dad asked. "It's hard, isn't it?"

I nodded yes. Mom and Dad understood my pain, because they shared it. I asked God to help me get through it. Slowly, I turned my thoughts to spring. The window was open, and I felt the fresh breeze and the warmth of the sun hit me as it shone through the window. I loved how everything was turning green. When we finally got home and settled in, Dad wanted to have a talk with all of us. We gathered around the table, and Dad said, "You all now know Randy is home to stay for good. He's still the same brother you've always had. He just happens to be in a wheelchair now. Treat him the same way you always have. He doesn't want to be treated special. He's not going to break, and he's not fragile. Don't treat him any differently. Okay?" My siblings all agreed, and from that moment on, I was always treated as their brother, Randy. I was never "Randy in the wheelchair." Starting from that moment, I never felt handicapped around them, something I always appreciated.

Indeed, it was good to be home. We were a family of seven again. The wishes and prayers of my parents and I had been fulfilled with my return home. I was truly blessed with a wonderful family. "You were the family project," Mom later explained. This was a lovable phrase for her as she tried to emphasize how my accident brought us closer together. I've always gained strength from their support of me.

CHAPTER 24
THIS CAN'T BE HAPPENING!

"I can do all things through Christ
who strengthens me."
—Philippians 4:13

When I'd been home for three weeks, the one year anniversary of my accident drew near. Everything was going smoothly at home, so I didn't think about it much. We had established a routine. Mom got up early to do my bed bath, and bowel care each day before work. Then, I'd fall back to sleep for a little while until Dad, Jim, and Bob would get me dressed and into my chair. I sat on a cushion that had air in it. It wasn't filled full of air because it would then be too hard to sit on. The cushion helped prevent pressure sores. My arms rested on the tray attached to the arms of my chair. The toggle switch, which allowed me to operate the chair, was swung around in front of my mouth.

Once this was taken care of, I had a bit more freedom. I could move on my own by operating the toggle switch with my mouth and tongue. It was simple. I used my tongue to lift up on the switch to go forward, push down to go backward, push left to go left, and right to go right.

In fact, all of my siblings helped me with my cares. Mom and Dad did the majority, but as time went on, Jim helped get me in and out of bed, Becky and Linda washed my hair, and Bob helped with my range of motion therapy. And, whenever needed, someone in the family would empty the urine bag strapped to my leg. It was no big deal to any of us. And I never felt any resentment on their part. In return, I tried to help the family too. I'd help my brothers and sisters with their homework, and Mom had me make certain things got done around the house when she was at work. I'll never forget how Linda and I would get the mail. I'd wheel down our long dirt driveway with Linda either following along or sometimes riding on the battery box of my wheelchair. Linda couldn't reach the mailbox because she was too short, so she'd crawl up on my chair. She'd open the box, grab the mail, and back to the house we'd go.

It was great being together as a family again. From time to time, my thoughts wandered back to First East. How were my fellow patients, aides, therapists, and so many more hospital staff members doing? I couldn't forget about them. But I wrote to many of them and kept in touch to maintain our ties.

Indeed, everything was going well. We even continued our family tradition of going to the outdoor theater when it opened for the summer. We all were so excited. I don't remember the movie, only that it was a John Wayne western. Mom popped her usual big brown bag of popcorn for us to share during the movie. We got situated in the car and headed to the theater. I was sitting in the front seat by the passenger door, Mom was next to me, Dad was by the driver's door, and my siblings were in the back seat. Sometimes, Linda would crawl up to the front seat. After we'd been there for a while, Mom reached down to place my right ankle over my left one to relieve pressure off of my right heel. Shortly after my accident, when I started having muscle spasms, my legs would contract. This made my heels rub against the sheet, causing a red, tender area only on my right heel. We kept a close eye on it to make sure it didn't get any worse. But this time, when Mom moved my right ankle over my left one, there was a snapping sound as though someone had taken a dry twig and broke it in half. It was very loud. Everyone in the car heard it. "What was that?" asked Jim. The snapping sound came from my right leg, but we didn't know what it was. "Are you okay?" asked Mom.

I wasn't in any pain, and everything felt like usual, so I said, "I think so." We watched the rest of the movie without any real concerns.

When I was transferred from the chair to my bed that night, something seemed different. Although I always had leg spasms when being transferred, this time my right leg didn't kick out as far as usual. I noticed, but didn't tell anyone. It was then that I began to think something was wrong with my right leg. That night, I prayed to God and asked Him to let my leg be all right. Mom must have noticed something too, because early the next morning, she said, "Randy, we're going to take you to the emergency room to make sure everything is okay with your leg."

I knew my leg needed to be checked, so I wasn't upset or disappointed. We got in the car and headed to the Austin ER. When we got there, my parents explained the situation to the doctor.

"I'm sure it's not broken," he said, "but we'll take an X-ray just in case."

It didn't take long, and when I got back to Mom and Dad, we commenced waiting in a very small room for the doctor to return. It seemed to take forever. When he came back, he said, "Randy has a broken leg, right above the knee in his femur."

I couldn't believe it! I thought something might be wrong, but I never thought my leg was broken!

"We can't take care of it here, so we're going to send him by ambulance to St. Marys Hospital in Rochester," said the doctor. "I called them, and they are expecting him."

I was stunned. Mom apologized, but I assured her it was not her fault. Mom planned to ride in the ambulance with me. Dad said he'd meet us there. Within minutes, we were headed back to St. Marys. I was scared and unsure what to think. All I knew was that this was another obstacle to face in my journey.

Chapter 25
Familiar Territory

"We also rejoice in our sufferings, because we know that suffering produces perseverance; perseverance, character; and character, hope."
—Romans 5:3–4

When we arrived at St. Marys, we pulled into the same ER garage that we had exactly one year ago, after my accident. It was hard to believe it had been twelve months since I had broken my neck. Now, here I was in the same ER with a broken leg.

Dad wasn't far behind the ambulance, and when he arrived, this time, they let me see him. I thought they'd just fix my leg and I'd go back home. I wasn't expecting to stay overnight. But I was very wrong. A doctor came in and said, "We want to take some more X-rays to see exactly what we're dealing with. Do you have any questions first?" When none of us did, the doctor said, "I'll be back after we get the X-rays."

I was lying on my back with my broken leg propped up on a pillow. I was comfortable and not in any pain, which made it even more difficult to understand that there could be something wrong. But as I lay there, my heart ached for Mom. I knew she felt this situation was her fault for moving my leg, but it wasn't. She was just trying to help me out, doing something she'd done before. "Everything will be okay," I said when I noticed her distress. She just shook her head.

As with so many other times in the hospital setting, our wait took quite a while. When the doctor finally arrived, he said, "The X-rays show it's a clean break, but now we need to figure out what kind of cast would work the best. We need to take into account your paralysis. I talked to Dr. Jackson, and we've decided to put on a cast that can be opened up depending on which position you are in while lying in bed. Someone will be coming to get you shortly to put your cast on."

We thanked the doctor, still not knowing what it would mean. When they came to cast me, they used a plaster type material from my right hip down to my foot. It took thirty to forty-five minutes to dry, after which, they cut the cast open along each side, putting straps around it to secure it in place. This way, they could remove part of the cast depending on my position. When the staff had finished, I returned to the ER room where Mom and Dad were waiting. The doctor came in and said, "You'll be going to a room on First East—the rehab floor. They can meet your needs best there. I'm sure you're familiar with it."

My heart sank as two things hit me: first, that I'd be staying overnight and second, that I was going to First East, which usually meant a lengthy hospital stay. I was disappointed. Mom, Dad, and I headed up to First East. On the way, Mom tried to look at the bright side and said, "You'll probably see some of the friends you met when you were here before."

"Probably," I muttered. I knew it would be nice to see them, but I was concerned about staying in the hospital when I wanted to be home. As soon as we got to First East, just about everyone said, "Hi, Randy!" It was good to see them, but I wished the circumstances were different. They placed me in a different room than before. Not many faces had changed in the past month, so it was nice to have people do my cares who were familiar with me. For the first time, they had me lay on my stomach so the back part of my leg could be exposed. A towel was rolled up and placed under my forehead to keep my face from being buried in the mattress. This was hard on my neck and made it difficult to breathe. We tried this for a few days, but it became quite evident it wasn't going to work. I felt panic being in this position. My neck ached, but the fear of suffocation rushed back. It returned me to the tracheotomy being plugged. I didn't want to go through the suffocating fears again. I felt helpless, and hope seemed far away. Thankfully, the doctors decided to try a different cast called a spica cast. It mobilizes the hips and thighs to help with the healing process. The spica cast ran from the toes on my right leg up to my chest. About the only things that weren't covered were my head and left leg. I was immobilized in my bed or on a cart. Lying there, I couldn't believe this was happening to me. I prayed for God to help me and grant me strength to get through it.

Those days back on First East were some of the longest I'd ever spent there. The healing process was lengthy and slow. I had too much time to think. So many thoughts were running through my mind. How long would it take for my leg to heal? How long would I be in hospital? What were my siblings thinking? How would Mom and Dad make it through this ordeal and keep the family together? I was now a year older and had grown more sensitive to how my situation affected others. I worried about their feelings sometimes more than my own. I knew my siblings longed for the security of family as much as I did.

A few years later, Becky said, "When you got hurt, you took our mother away from us for a while." I didn't know what to say. All I could say was, "I'm sorry." That was the end of the conversation. Her words cut right to my heart. I had no idea my siblings felt this way. I asked each of them, "Please be honest with me. Do you feel I took Mom away from you when I broke my neck?" They all said, "No, we knew you were very sick and thought you needed Mom with you." This was a huge relief, but Becky's words still hurt. I don't believe she told me to hurt me. I'm glad she felt comfortable enough to tell me this. It may have been healing to Becky to share those feelings with me. It was also a gift to me, so I could realize how my accident impacted others. My accident happened to me physically, but it happened to my family too. When I broke my neck the year prior, I focused mostly on my own confusion and pain. Now, I was worried about what my situation would do to those I loved.

Therapy was limited. Range of motion in PT was all I could do—and even that was limited, as they had to be careful not to disturb my broken leg so it could heal. Even though my surroundings were familiar, I had such a different care plan than the time I was on First East before. I didn't have OT because I was confined to my bed or a cart. And school was no longer in session, which meant the days dragged on. The only highlight was when Mom came to see me after work. Still, I wasn't sure I could emotionally handle another long hospital stay. The darkness set in again. Unlike with my broken neck, I knew what was ahead. The hospital stay would be long, I wouldn't see my siblings, and being away from home was pushing me over the edge. I felt more pain and anger. The only person I ever vented to was Mom. "Mom, I'm not sure I can deal with this!" I expressed hurtfully.

"Randy, we'll make it through," she said reassuringly. I didn't feel as comforted by her words as usual. The pain was deeper than I ever felt. All it amounted to was a waiting game. Being hospitalized again nearly overwhelmed me at times. I wasn't sure I'd make it. This was easily the darkest period I've ever lived through. I tried venting to Mom, but I couldn't let the full extent of my pain out. I kept it buried deep inside. About the only thing that kept me going during this setback was my family and prayer. I turned to God for much needed strength. I talked to Him as though He were there with me, having a one-on-one conversation. One night, early on, I prayed with tears running down my cheeks, "God, I'm not sure I can make it through this. I need some strength and peace from you. The only way I can do it is with your love. God, please give me hope. Keep my family safe and let them know I'll always love them. I miss them so much! Help me because I'm afraid and scared. I love you! Amen." It was a relief to express my raw emotions. I felt connected with God more than ever.

The next day, I felt an entirely new sense of peace wash over me. I had given my fears to the Lord, and He heard me. So many of my fears and burdens were lifted from my shoulders that day. I had simply given it up to Him. After, I never felt alone at night when the lights were turned out because I turned to God in prayer. And each night, He answered my prayers in the peace and calmness that overcame me after. I loved this feeling. I knew everything would be okay.

One day, after three months in the hospital, my parents were visiting me when Dr. Jackson and his associates came in. "We are going to take an X-ray of your leg, Randy, to see how it's healing," said Dr. Jackson.

"It doesn't need to be healing perfectly, since he'll never walk on it again," said an associate quickly. This comment only heightened my broken leg fears. Perhaps she thought this would comfort me, knowing I could go home sooner. This seemed rather insensitive to me. I was shocked by it, and so was Dad.

"How do you know he'll never walk on it again?" asked my Dad in anger. "You can't say that for sure. You never should've said that! I can't believe you just said that in front of my son. That was wrong and inappropriate!"

There was dead silence.

Dad had a hard time accepting the fact that I would be in a wheelchair for the rest of my life. He was lashing out to protect me and keep my hopes, as well as his, alive.

After a minute, the associate apologized, "You're right. I shouldn't have said that. I'm sorry."

Then, Dr. Jackson reached out, shook Dad's hand, and said, "We'll get that X-ray taken today." Dr. Jackson never came to the defense of his associate that day, but an important lesson was learned by everyone about not giving up hope and using appropriate terminology.

In the end, the X-rays showed my leg was healing just fine. This was welcome news, since the summer was almost over, meaning it was time for school to start soon. I had mixed feelings about this. School meant my day would get busier, which I was glad about. On the flip side, I now knew my hospital stay would last a while longer because they were setting up eighth grade tutoring for me. Luckily, I had the same tutors as I did the year prior, and with the addition of school, time went by faster. On First East, the faces had changed some, but the changes were gradual. Some of my fellow patients had gone home, and there were new aides walking the halls. This time around, I didn't feel as close to the new patients and staff members. The family atmosphere wasn't as strong. Perhaps I had my guard up, thinking I'd be going home sooner.

By October, five months of this hospital stay passed. I kept wondering how much longer I'd have to be there, but never once did I ask. Fortunately, in mid-October, Dr. Jackson came in and said, "We'll be taking all but your leg cast off tomorrow. We'll see how that goes, which I think will be fine, and then you can try going home for a couple weekends and then home for good in a few weeks."

This was good news, and it seemed to come out of the blue. I thanked God. All went well with the cast removal. I was then able to sit up in my chair for a while. Everyone was happy for me.

"Randy, the staff can't believe how much you've been through and that you've still managed to keep your spirits high," said Mom.

"Mom, all the patients have been through a lot, not just me," I said.

Two weeks later, I was able to return home on weekends. The rest of my cast was removed toward late November, and I was released from the hospital by early December. Of the past eighteen months, I'd spent seventeen of them in the hospital. This time, it wasn't as hard to say good-bye.

CHAPTER 26
HOME FOR GOOD—AGAIN

"I will instruct you and teach you in the way you should go. I will counsel you with my eye upon you."
—Psalm 32:8

At home, we picked up where we left off before my broken leg. It was good to be where everything was familiar. Dad's work clothes still hung in the entryway. The house still smelled like Mom's cooking and fragrant crafts. Outside, you could smell the barn, the feed, the milkers, and the manure. In short, it all smelled like home.

Here, and nowhere else, was that feeling of security that you gain from being part of a strong family unit. We were one again, and there were smiles everywhere. Everything was simpler when we were together. The stress level was much lower for my parents. They no longer made the commute to Rochester, which meant more time with all five kids, and the familiar routine of daily farm life was back in order. Miraculously, the family made it through the trauma of my accident and remained strong. "We simply did what we had to do," said Mom. "We had no choice." But, the truth is, they did have a choice, and they chose to put family first. My parents sacrificed a lot to keep the family together. My mom and dad were thirty-eight and forty-one respectively at the time of my accident. Their social life was on hold. They didn't even spend much time together with Mom at the hospital so much. How did their marriage survive this life-changing incident? During my hospital stay, we had witnessed firsthand the number of families and relationships that fell apart under the stress of illness and recovery. Many people simply couldn't accept and deal with a life-changing accident like mine. Mom and Dad didn't think; they just did. They put everyone's needs ahead of their own. Even my siblings were great through it all. They were supportive of me and treated me no differently. They helped me and tended to my needs, and I tried to help them in whatever ways I was able. It was the least I could do. As a family, we used the accident as an opportunity to draw closer together. It was, clearly, God's ultimate gift to my family: to take what could have been a tragedy and turn it into a triumph.

Once back home, life settled into routine after my birthday and Christmas, my first at home in two years. The tutors from the hospital and school had set up my schedule so I'd be tutored at home once Christmas vacation was done. They came directly to the farm around 3:30 p.m., after they finished teaching at school. We sat at a card table in the living room, and my siblings knew this was off-limits during my tutoring. Through one-on-one learning, I studied math, English, social studies, and science during intensive two hour sessions. Mom and Dad got me an electric typewriter for homework. I'd wheel up to the dining room table, and a family member would pull it onto my tray. I was soon typing twenty-five words per minute, which is pretty good with mouthsticks. The keys were easy to push, but for some reason, the backspace was difficult. I was careful not to make mistakes. Computers eventually simplified this. Learning at home was a great opportunity, but I really missed the classroom atmosphere and friendships and camaraderie.

As the school year progressed, and I was busy soaking up all of the knowledge I could, I relished the farm routine as well. There was something comforting in knowing the animals had to be fed at the same time each day and that Dad would milk the cows at the same time in the morning and evening.

As the winter of 1968 approached, I knew it would be a time I wouldn't get out much. Winter made it difficult to navigate. And that winter in particular was an unusual one in Minnesota, with an abundance of snow and bitter temperatures. I no longer cared for the colder temperatures, whereas before my accident, I looked forward to the snow. Now, my spinal cord injury had affected my body thermostat. I was cold all of the time. I dreamed of summer and couldn't wait to sit outside, with the warmth of the sun blanketing me. Over time, sitting in the wheelchair wore away my body and joints, causing extensive arthritis. The sun became a salve, soothing my pain and refreshing my soul.

But before too long, spring arrived, and with it, the promise of summer. At fourteen, I would be a freshman in junior high school in the fall. The second year anniversary of my accident was also approaching. In some ways, it felt like it flew by because I hadn't been home for most of those two years. All that time in the hospital seemed like another lifetime. We didn't talk about it much, but we didn't ignore it either. On the other hand, it seemed much longer than two years. Now was a time of reflection.

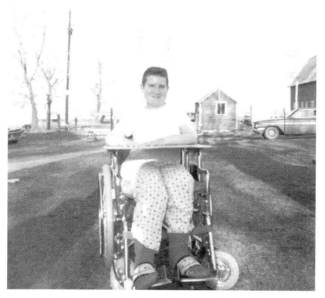

Home on the farm for good! (1968)

It had been a long journey, but when I thought about it, I had also become a much different person. I had been through much more than others my own age and was now thankful that I had walked that path. I was blessed to live two lives. The first twelve years, I was an active boy. I couldn't have asked for a better first part of life. The second part was entirely different. I was limited physically, but every experience of my new lifestyle opened my eyes. I witnessed firsthand the pain and suffering others endured. It hurt me knowing they were hurting. I had always been sensitive, the type of kid who felt bad for those picked last to be on teams. When I got to be a team captain, I picked those kids about halfway through. Their faces lit up. It was better than winning. That sensitivity helped me relate to others who may be hurting. In fact, everything I saw, felt, and experienced over those two years after my accident helped me grow in compassion. That growth applied to all areas of my life. It shaped who I am today. I became able to see things differently—to see the good in the bad, the joy in the sorrow. I saw and felt God everywhere.

CHAPTER 27
FAMILY

*"Trust in the Lord with all your heart, and
do not lean on your own understanding.
In all your ways, acknowledge him,
and he will make straight your paths."*
—Proverbs 3: 5–6

The summer of 1968 did not go by very fast. Farm life is difficult, involving lots of hard work. It's a slower paced lifestyle, which was in stark contrast to my old routine on First East, where everything was structured and regimented. We did a lot that summer at home. I'd watch everyone do their chores, spend time with them when they played games, go fishing, and more. I spent most of my time outside and loved every minute of it. I took in all the gifts God had waiting for me.

I also grew even closer to my siblings, but especially to Bob and Linda. Like all siblings, we had our disagreements, but they never lasted long. Jim was busy helping Dad with farm chores, and Becky was helping out in the house. She also played with her friends a lot and spent time in her playhouse. Bob would soon take on an expanded role helping with chores, but that summer he had a lot of spare time. Bob, Linda, and I formed a very strong bond. We loved each other dearly. In particular, Bob and I have very similar personalities. Like me, he's a quiet person who keeps his thoughts inside. Mom used to say, "The school could burn down, and I wouldn't find out from Bob."

Perhaps one of the reasons Bob and Linda and I bonded so well is that they didn't have much of a recollection of me before my accident. They grew up knowing me the way I am now. It was never a big deal to them. They never expected me to be anyone other than who I was, and they adapted to the situation easily. Once Bob was showing me something he'd found, and I asked, "Is it very heavy?" Without thought, Bob placed it on top of my head, gently steadied it, and asked, "Can you tell?"

"Yeah, I can!" I said with enthusiasm. It became a new way for us to communicate. From that moment on, everyone placed objects on top of my head so I could feel the weight.

During Linda's high school years and after, she and I grew particularly close. She was so involved in sports, and I'd coach her and give her a little extra shove from time to time. She responded well to this motivation and encouragement. When they were younger, the three of us would play games together, and I'd be their coach and commentator. These games consisted of basketball, softball, kickball, and more. We all enjoyed sports. Sometimes, we made up games. We had a very lightweight ball, about the size of a basketball, but much lighter. Since I couldn't play catch with them, I'd have them toss that ball toward my forehead, and I'd bounce it back to them. We also improvised a baseball type game. I was the batter, and they were the fielders. Each team got three outs. The ball would bounce off my head, and if one of them caught it, then it would be an out, but if it hit the ground, it was a hit. I grew so adept at this game that I'd angle my head different ways to make the ball go in different directions. Whenever one of them would make a great catch, I'd praise them. I wanted to help build their self-esteem because it makes people believe in themselves even more. Then, they try even harder.

"If you're going to do something, always give it all you have," I'd encourage. I hated seeing people rob themselves by not giving it their all. I knew how precious life was and that it can all be taken from you in an instant. I always encouraged others to give it all they had and, that way, they'd never have regrets. Bob and Linda did give it their all. They accepted my motivation and mentoring. They connected with me and understood where I was coming from.

Beck was starting her adolescence. We listened to the radio and talked about her friends that summer. We too had a strong bond. Beck and I laughed about times before my accident. We reflected on riding our bikes, playing in the snow, and much more. I could sense she was growing up. Jim and I spent time together that summer too. I'd talk with him about chores, hunting, and the 4-H softball team. He shared the team practices and games with me. We both enjoyed playing 4-H softball. I was happy to hear they had another good team.

That summer of 1968 was also the summer Mom and Dad got a Volkswagen van to make it easier for me to be transported. Dad had built two metal ramps, one for each side of my chair. The van doors would be opened, and the ramps would be set on the floor of the van and lined up on the ground. The ramps needed to be placed just far enough apart so I could wheel right up into the van. Once I was in the van, the ramps were placed under my chair, up against my wheels. This kept my chair in place, and kept the ramps in the van should we need them at our destination.

Well, Jim had gotten his driver's license the previous summer. One Sunday, we were at my Grandma Krulish's (Dad's mom). Jim had a big league 4-H softball game that day, so he and I talked Mom and Dad into letting Jim drive me to the game. I had a great time! It was fun seeing so many friends from 4-H. But on the way back to Grandma's, Jim took a curve in the road too fast. My wheelchair tipped over against the van doors, causing them to fly open. My head and shoulders were hanging out of the van. From this vantage, I could see, right in front of my eyes, the front passenger's tire turning. It was truly frightening! When I saw that tire turning, I prayed, "God, help me!"

The ramps kept me from falling forward or backward, but not sideways. Jim stopped the van as fast as he could and rushed over to me. "Are you okay?!" he shouted, fear in his eyes.

"Yeah, I think so," I said. His eyes were tearing up. He was starting to panic.

Staying calm, I said, "I'm fine. Do you think you can get me back in my chair?"

And, somehow, he got me and the wheelchair back into an upright position. He was crying as he got me positioned in my chair. "You're doing a great job!" I said.

After he got me situated, he asked, "Do you feel okay?"

"Yeah, you got me sitting great!" I said. "Don't worry. Everything is fine."

He was sure we would be in big trouble with our parents, so we decided not to tell them. Jim took the time to calm down before we went back to Grandma's. We acted as if everything was fine. Soon, it was time to go home to milk the cows. That night, when I was being put into bed, Dad saw a bruise on my right shoulder. "What's this from?" he asked.

Knowing we couldn't hide it any longer, we spilled the beans. All Dad said was, "Jim, you have to be more careful driving the van."

"Are you sure you feel okay?" Mom asked me repeatedly. I finally convinced her everything was fine.

Indeed, that was a memory neither Jim nor I ever forgot. It helped us grow even closer. Even though unspoken, we would always be there for one another.

The summer of 1968 was memorable in many ways, but perhaps the most important part of that summer was how our family grew together. It was a new start for us. We were all journeying, as a family of one, along this unexpected path after my accident. We were learning about the blessings that the accident, while initially tragic, had bestowed on us, such as our family support. No matter what happened, we remained family. We loved one another, and encouraged each other to be the best that we could.

CHAPTER 28
ADAPTING TO MY NEW LIFE

"I know the plans I have for you,
says the Lord, plans to prosper you,
to give you a hope and future."
—Jeremiah 29:11

Getting back into the routine of home and family was an easy adjustment that year. It was there, where I felt most safe and secure, that I was also forced to evaluate the tougher stuff. The psychological aspect of dealing with paralysis is much more difficult. Acceptance was easy. The accident happened; there was nothing I could do to change that. Adjusting to it was something altogether different. After a while, I was forced to accept my physical limitations. Sitting back watching everyone do their activities hurt—it saddened me. I knew I'd never drive a tractor, do chores, or throw a softball again. There were so many things, simple things. I'd watch Jim or Bob mow the lawn and think, *I'd love to do that!* It wore on me mentally and emotionally. I never shared those feelings with anyone except God.

Each day was the same. I'd get in my wheelchair every morning, and the day passed in routine. It didn't change, which made it easier to handle. But there were periodic setbacks or reminders. For example, many places weren't handicapped accessible. Sometimes we made plans to go somewhere, and then found out our destination wasn't accessible. This tested my faith. To be honest, I don't recall seeing people in wheelchairs out and about before my accident, either. They just stayed in their homes and didn't go out into society. I decided this had to change. I didn't want to stay cooped up day in and day out, and I doubted others did either. When we moved to a different farm in 1969 in the Lyle school district, I had to continue going to the Austin school I was attending, because it had a freight elevator and Lyle didn't. This was disappointing for me. Another adjustment was needed.

My parents were my biggest supporters. The portable ramps Dad made helped solve some of the problems. But sometimes I got to a store just fine and went in, only to be unable to move farther because the aisles were narrow and had boxes blocking them. And people stared. If I hadn't been familiar with my own situation, I might have stared too. Sometimes, kids would approach me, point at the toggle switch, and ask, "What's that?" or "What happened to you?"

This excited me. Someone was seeing me! Someone cared enough to ask! But as I started to tell them, a parent would grab them by the hand and say, "Leave him alone." They'd walk away without talking to me. Those kids were only curious, and I wanted to tell them. They needed to know. There was no handicapped awareness, and I thought the only way they'd learn was by asking and being told by someone who knew. The parents made me feel like I was so different. I felt unwelcome. It felt as though they thought my paralysis was contagious.

Infrequently, we'd go to a restaurant, and the waitress would come to take our order. When she got to me, she'd ask Mom or Dad while pointing at me, "What does he want?" She didn't think I could talk. Either I'd just start speaking for myself, or Dad would say, "Ask him." This probably made her feel uncomfortable, but at least she found out I could talk. People saw me differently than able-bodied people. But I was a human being with feelings, like anyone else. I didn't like being different.

Sometimes my aunts, uncles, and cousins stopped by to visit. But our relationships were never the same. My cousins were always nice to me, but with some, there was an awkward and uncomfortable feeling that hadn't been present before. I don't think they knew how to treat me. It's like they were walking on eggshells. They were unsure of what to say or how to act. They seemed to have their guard up around me. On the other hand, some cousins treated me the same and wanted to protect me. I always appreciated that. I just wanted to be treated like the same Randy.

It felt this way at school too. My friends thought because I had changed physically that they should treat me differently. They stared. It wasn't blatant, more like a quick stare, glance away, and stare again. I hated this. It made me feel different, and I didn't want to be different.

My parents did a wonderful job of making me feel like a member of the family and not handicapped. Whenever someone did treat me the same as before the accident, I appreciated it so much. Mom and Dad once told me that after my accident, many family members and friends asked, "How's Randy doing?"

My parents would answer, "He's doing well. He's having therapy and getting better."

"Yeah, but how's his mind?" they'd ask. "Can he still think okay?"

This bothered my parents. But they always answered, "His mind is fine. He's as smart as he's always been. The accident affected him physically, not mentally."

This story was an eye-opener for me. I had no idea people linked my paralysis to my mental state. People assumed so many things because there wasn't enough awareness about physically handicapped people. It was for this reason that I felt most comfortable at home with my family or among friends from First East. My siblings were also completely aware of my situation. They were always looking out for me. On field trips, they'd look for handicapped accessibility and come home excited to tell me, "Randy, you could get in the building because it doesn't have steps." I was so happy they were thinking of me.

School was about to start, so I filed the handicapped awareness thoughts in the back of my mind. Now it was time to focus on my education!

CHAPTER 29
BACK TO SCHOOL

*"Give thanks in all circumstances; for this is
the will of God in Christ Jesus for you."*
—1 Thessalonians 5:18

As the summer of 1968 came to an end, a new chapter in my life was beginning. I was going to be in ninth grade, my final year in junior high school. It was strange to think of myself as a freshman. As I was making that transition, Linda was entering kindergarten. All of the Krulish kids would now be in school.

In August, Mom contacted Ellis Junior High, the school I would've attended, to set up my tutoring schedule. A few days later, we were surprised to learn that the principal, Mr. Tyler, wanted to meet with us. None of us knew why, but I didn't dwell on it too long. I was just excited to step foot in a school again. The last time I'd actually been in a school was sixth grade, right before my accident. When we arrived at the school for our visit, we entered through the back door, the only handicapped accessible entrance. The custodian was there, since this was his area. He gave us directions to the principal's office. After introductions and handshakes, Mr. Tyler asked my parents to have a seat. I liked him immediately. He was very friendly and had an ear-to-ear smile. After we were all settled and pleasantries exchanged, Mr. Tyler got right to the heart of the matter.

"I've been thinking about something and wanted to get your views on it," he began. "I'd like to work something out so Randy could come here for school this year. What do you think of that, Randy?"

I was in shock, but I managed to answer, "I'd love that!"

"What do you think?" Mr. Tyler asked my parents.

Given our experiences with the general lack of acceptance and understanding of the handicapped, we were all taken off guard.

"If we could work all of the details out, I think it would be good for Randy," said Mom.

"We'd need to work out transportation and any other cares he'd need done for the day," agreed the principal.

"I can bring him to school every day, and pick him up," Dad volunteered.

I was so excited. I couldn't believe I'd be going to school this year—to the actual physical building. I was just thrilled! Again, my thoughts went right to thanking God for His goodness.

"What other cares would need to be done?" asked Mr. Tyler.

"Well, he'd need someone to feed him," said Mom. "And empty the urine from his leg bag."

"I'm sure the nurse can empty Randy's leg bag, and it shouldn't be a problem finding someone to feed him," he said. "One other concern I have is the motorized wheelchair. I wouldn't want someone to mess with any of the switches. Do you have a regular wheelchair?"

"Yeah," I said. "It's a manual one that needs to be pushed."

"I think we can find someone to help with that," he said, and he continued looking directly at me. "Randy, we know you're an excellent student. Do you think you could handle coming to school?"

"Yeah, I'm pretty sure I can," I said.

"I'm going to check into a couple things then, and I'll get back in touch with you," he said.

As we thanked him and said our good-byes, Mr. Tyler said, "Randy, I think we can work things out so you'll be the first physically handicapped student mainstreamed back into the Austin school district."

On the ride home, I was excited, and so were my parents. "I can't believe I'm going back to school!" I said.

"We think it's great for you, too, Randy! You'll be back with your classmates," said Mom.

"I know. I can't wait!" Then I added, "What does *mainstreamed* mean?" I wasn't quite sure what it meant, but it sounded like a good thing.

Mom answered, "When someone has an accident like yours, many times they just stay home and don't go back into society. Now, you'll be mainstreamed back into the school system."

Dad added, "With you going back to school, it'll show other kids they can return to school too if they have an accident or are sick for a long time."

"Am I the first one to do this?" I asked.

"In this school district, yes," said Mom.

It made me feel good to know that I would be helping others by paving the way for handicapped students to go back to school.

The next day, the principal called and told Mom about the schedule he'd worked out. At school, a custodian would wheel me to my first class and feed me at lunch. In my first class, the teacher would select a student to wheel me to the next class. This would be repeated with each class, until the final one. At the end of the day, a custodian would get me from that class and take me to the custodian work area, where Dad would be waiting to pick me up. My classmate helpers and I would get to leave each class a few minutes early to avoid the hallways when they were flooded with students heading to their next class. There would be times, though, we wouldn't make it ahead of the mad rush and, instead, we'd have to maneuver through the crowd to the next class. Since I couldn't take notes, the teachers also would appoint fellow classmates to give me a carbon copy of their notes. The teachers would give all tests to me orally. The school nurse would empty my leg bag down in the custodian work area while I ate lunch.

In the end, the details were trivial. I didn't really care, because what was important was that I was going back to school. I was overcome with joy and gratefulness. It hadn't crossed my mind I'd be going back to school. I just assumed I'd be tutored. I learned to quit assuming and to start enjoying. Now I was thrilled.

CHAPTER 30
ADJUSTING TO SCHOOL

"They are to do good, to be rich in good works, to be generous and ready to share."
—1 Timothy 6:18

When the first day of school finally arrived, I was prepared. This was my final year of junior high, and I had all of the necessary items—both the traditional ones every student needed and the ones only I would need, like a urinal into which the nurse would empty my leg bag. I was very nervous. I wondered what the kids would be like. Would they stare? Would they be friendly? Or would they treat me differently? There was so much that was unknown. The only thing I knew for certain was that I was happy to be back.

That morning, Dad helped me into the van. As we drove down the long, gravel, country road toward school, the dust billowed up in clouds. Dad asked, "Are you ready to go back?" And I was. I thought it would be fun. Dad agreed. Since he was a farmer and therefore his own boss, he was able to flex his schedule so he could take me to and from school. I saw this as a sign that God was paving the way for me to go back to school. Those trips with Dad to and from school became our special time. I'd had the opportunity to create a special bond with my siblings and Mom after my accident. This was my time with Dad, who never showed much emotion but was a fantastic storyteller who loved to laugh. In many ways, he was one of my biggest supporters. He wanted what was best for me, and I knew that without it ever being said. On the trips to school, Dad and I talked about school, family, sports, and much more.

On that first day back, Dad pulled up to the back entrance of the school and took me into the custodian's room. The custodians, who I would grow to know well, introduced themselves. We chatted awhile until John, a kindhearted soul who would help me most of the time, said, "We'd better get you to your first class."

"Have a good day," said Dad. "I'll pick you up when you're done."

John pushed me to English class, where I was placed next to a desk. The teacher welcomed me and introduced me to the classmates who'd take notes for me and help get me to the next class. We said our hellos. This was repeated with each class: algebra, history, science, and speech. And each time, I'd look around the room, and no one looked familiar. In all of my classes, there was only one classmate with whom I'd attended grade school. I was a little disappointed, but thought it would be a good opportunity to meet new friends. Everyone seemed nice.

After the third class, my helper wheeled me to the custodian's area so I could eat lunch. John did a good job feeding me. We talked about sports and the farm since he also grew up on one. The nurse emptied my leg bag. It wouldn't need to be emptied again until I got home. After lunch, John took me to my next class. Throughout the day, I had a chance to get to know the various helpers. We didn't get a chance to talk a lot because we were always in a hurry to get to my next class, but each was friendly. I always thanked them, and they seemed genuinely pleased and happy to help. One of them explained how he volunteered. "We met with the principal, and he asked if we could help you out. We all wanted to help. Besides, I get out of class a few minutes early," he said with a chuckle. This made me laugh too.

My last class was a study hall, which allowed me to go home an hour early. Dad was waiting for me. "How'd school go?" he asked.

"Great!" I replied. Dad smiled, loaded me into the van, and we headed for home. "What did you do in school?"

"I met my teachers and got my books. I also met the classmates who'll be helping me with notes and taking me to my classes. They seem like really nice guys."

"Did you thank them?" said Dad, asking his standard question.

"Yes, I did."

On the way home, I prayed in thanksgiving to God for letting me go back to school. I knew none of it would have been possible without the strength and support He gave me. The drive also gave me time to reflect on my first day inside a school in over two years. Overall, it had been a good day. Yes, there were stares and long looks. I felt the heat of them more than I witnessed them. It was something I'd grown to expect, as I'd experienced them often. For many kids, I was the first person they had seen in a wheelchair. I didn't let this bother me. I felt like I was doing some good. I believed once they got used to seeing me in the classrooms and hallways, the stares would subside.

"I wonder what Linda will say about her first day of kindergarten," Dad asked, interrupting my thoughts.

"It'll be fun hearing her talk about it!" I said. I could just picture Linda's enthusiasm on her first day of school. I was excited to get home and hear what my brothers and sisters thought about their days.

At home, when Dad asked Linda how she liked kindergarten, all she said was, "Good." She was home now and just wanted to go outside and play. Jim, now a senior, said his final year was "pretty much like any other." Popular Becky, now out of grade school and starting seventh grade, seemed excited and was anxious about starting more activities. Bob didn't say much of anything about being in third grade. In typical Bob fashion, he just went with the flow. When Mom got home, she wanted to hear about our days too. I told her how much I enjoyed being back in school.

Everyone seemed happy that day. We were in the swing of things as a family. There was comfort in knowing we were there for each other and interested in what each was experiencing. My accident had been a turning point in more ways than one. It definitely brought us closer, but it did so in an unexpected way. I learned, during my hospitalization and rehab, to put God first in my life. I struggled knowing my family would have to be second. But, ironically, once I made that step to put God first, the relationships I had with my family members grew stronger and became better than ever.

CHAPTER 31
SCHOOL DAYS

"Even though I walk through the valley of the shadow of death, I will fear no evil, for you are with me; your rod and your staff, they comfort me."
—Psalm 23:4

The rest of my freshman year went by smoothly. I enjoyed being back in school. The teachers were kind and seemed in-tune to my needs as a quadriplegic. I appreciated the extra effort they gave to make sure I could be there. Tests were given to me orally in the hallway by the door of our classroom. This way, the teacher could give me my test and still keep an eye on the other kids. I was blessed to get good grades. My name was printed in the Austin newspaper with other honor students. Mom, Dad, and additional family members made a big deal out of this, which made me feel good.

Eventually, the stares of curiosity that had been present at the beginning of school disappeared. People no longer glared as my helpers and I left class early. I became just another student. Still, something was missing. I didn't feel a close connection with my classmates the way I did throughout grade school. I had no time to socialize. I didn't participate in extracurricular activities, and I had no downtime to spend with them. Dad took me to school. The custodians took me to my first class. The helpers took me to the next. The custodians fed me lunch.

Dad picked me up when I was done. Nowhere in there was there time for interacting with students before, during, or after school. While I was thrilled to be in school, I couldn't help be disappointed that it wasn't what I remembered or expected. I'd hear my siblings talk about their friends and I yearned for the same.

I struggled sometimes with feeling different. It didn't help that I couldn't always control my body. In science class one day, the teacher was giving a lecture when I had a muscle spasm that straightened out my left arm and knocked my book and book holder to the floor. Typically, my right hand was straight out in front of me, resting on my tray, and my left arm was in against my stomach, allowing for plenty of room for my book and book holder. When my left arm knocked those items to the floor, there was complete silence. All eyes were on me. The student next to me bent over to pick them up and placed them back on my tray. I could hear the whispers. I felt conspicuous. Junior high is where you want to blend in and not stand out. I wanted to explain what happened to everyone, that it was normal for me to have spasms, but my teacher continued with his lecture as if nothing had happened. While this incident was quickly forgotten, I felt embarrassed.

At the end of the year, Jim graduated, marking a significant change in our lives. We were all growing up and maturing. I realized things would be different for me as time advanced. Jim was busy with his friends and school activities when he wasn't helping on the farm. Becky was active too. At times, they both were thoughtful and included me in their activities, but many nights I found myself staying home with Bob and Linda. This occasionally hurt and even angered me. I knew my life would be different, but I never thought I'd feel so lonely. Sometimes the tears would return in the middle of the night. I couldn't expect others to entertain me, but I missed the social experience I'd come to know before my accident. This was my life now. It would be different from that of others. And yet, I had the same wants and desires as anyone my age had. I wanted to participate in sports, go out with friends, meet girls, and just do what other freshman kids did. For now, I buried the pain deep within my soul.

As a sophomore, I transitioned to the Austin high school. It was a very dark and drab facility. The setup for my classes was similar to my freshman year schedule. The only difference was that this school had a freight elevator to take me to the different floors. In junior high, all classes were on one floor.

After I had been in high school a few weeks, Roger, one of my helpers, was taking me to my next class when another student asked, "So, you're playing nursemaid today, huh?"

"Just be quiet," said Roger. "You don't know what you're talking about."

The other student laughed.

"Don't let him bother you," I told Roger. "It's not worth it."

I felt bad for Roger. I tried not to show it, but I could sense he knew those words hurt me. I've never understood why some people say hurtful things and make fun of what they don't understand. But high school can be a cruel time. Once again, I wanted to blend in and not stand out. It was difficult. My history teacher was announcing our test results one day—and she wasn't happy. "Class," she said, gaining our attention. "I'm very disappointed in you! Obviously, you didn't spend time studying. The only one who got a good grade is Randy." I wanted to crawl into a hole and hide. No one wants to be singled out in front of their peers, whether for something good or bad. To make matters worse, she added, "Randy can't even take his own notes. Maybe you could learn something from him." I prayed the other students wouldn't hold this against me. Acceptance is something we all strive for. I didn't want my classmates to think I was better than them. Thankfully, they were still nice, but I didn't feel I was fitting in. I even considered not trying so hard next time, but that was contrary to everything I'd ever been taught.

**Left to right - Jim, Mom, me, Becky, Linda,
and Dad – Bob taking picture (1970)**

In the end, my sophomore year passed quickly. And no matter how things went during the day, I could always return home to the sense of security my family offered. When my junior year began, I couldn't help wondering where the time had gone. Jim had moved into an apartment with a friend and was working at an implement factory, making grain elevators. Becky was a freshman and was quite popular with the guys, though she wasn't allowed to date yet. Bob was in fifth grade and doing fine in school. Linda was now a second grader and still a tomboy.

In school, I was taking some new classes. Aside from the basics, I also took Spanish, advanced algebra, speech, and a broadcasting class. I made the National Honor Society that year. My favorite class was broadcasting. It was the first year it was offered at school. I jumped at the chance to take it, in part because the teacher was one I really enjoyed. He was very nice and genuinely cared about his students. One of our class projects was to do a demonstration tape on any topic we wanted. I chose to do one on using my mouthstick. With the tape, I was able to show the freedom and independence the mouthstick gave me. The demo went really well. My teacher said it was the best demo done, which felt great. Toward the end of that year, my teacher asked, "Randy, would you mind if I showed your demo to next year's class?"

I was taken aback, but answered, "Yeah, I guess that would be okay." I was surprised he felt I had something to offer. I was filled with anxiety issues like most teens. I found out later that he showed my demo tape to each of his classes until he retired. Years later, strangers would approach me and say, "Are you Randy?" When I said yes, they'd say, "I saw your demo tape in broadcasting class. It was great to see all the things you can do. It was really inspiring!" This always amazed me. God had been using me to teach others about the abilities of the handicapped for years, and I didn't even know it.

When my senior year rolled around, my schedule was much the same, with the exception of my humanities class. One day, our assignment was to describe a diagram that we could only see for thirty seconds first. Our classmates had to draw the diagram after hearing our description. What was most unusual about this assignment was that we couldn't use our arms and hands. Guess you could say I had an advantage. I couldn't use my arms and hands, but I could talk. I was used to having to be very descriptive since I couldn't move my arms and hands to point. I may have lost the sense of touch, but my other senses were heightened. As it turned out, my classmates were able to draw my diagram without much trouble. Surprisingly, many classmates struggled with their descriptions.

**Left to right - Becky, Linda, me, Bob, and Jim –
getting ready for my graduation (1972)}>>**

As my senior year came to an end, graduation loomed. I couldn't help but reflect on my journey. Even though I'd had a traumatic accident and long path toward recovery, I was still able to graduate on time with my classmates in 1972. When I was wheeled across the stage to receive my diploma, it was by John, the custodian with whom I'd connected. He was just as proud as my family members.

Chapter 32
Where Do I Go From Here?

"As you come to him, a living stone rejected
by men but in the sight of God,
chosen and precious."
—1 Peter 2:4

Graduating high school was a great achievement, but I wanted to do more, to be more. I wanted to attend the University of Missouri at Columbia. Julie, my friend from First East at St. Marys, had attended that university to get her nursing degree. I'd stayed in touch with her over the years and learned that the entire campus was handicapped accessible. I applied and was excited when I received my acceptance letter.

My goal was to become a social worker and help others who might one day face a life-changing accident. I also wanted to study broadcasting. My high school adviser set me up with Mr. Fisher, a vocational rehab counselor, who helped get everything ready for me to go to the University of Missouri. His job was to help get me involved in a vocation. Mr. Fisher communicated with the university concerning my arrival and passed on particulars about my physical handicap. He also made sure vocational rehab had the funding to pay my tuition. Part of getting ready to go to college involved a trip to Columbia a few days before classes started to locate someone who could help with my cares. There were plenty of students looking to make some extra money. Mom came with me, and we found a nice guy named Adam who Mom trained to do my cares. Adam was also my dorm roommate, which worked out great. The residents in my dorm were mostly physically handicapped students and their attendants. Adam was a grad student at the university and familiar with the campus. He had been on the wrestling team and was a great athlete. His sister medaled for the United States in figure skating in the 1972 Winter Olympics. Since I love sports, we had a lot to talk about.

When Mom was satisfied Adam was schooled in my cares, she headed back home, and I was on my own—a college student at the University of Missouri. It was hard when she left. Inside, I had that same empty feeling that I had when she left First East every evening—only, this time, it was more significant because I knew she wouldn't be back the next day. In fact, I probably wouldn't see her or my family again until Thanksgiving. The security of my family life was now four hundred miles away. I worried about getting my cares done properly and was nervous about being alone for the first time in my life. I wasn't alone, though. There were other students who were or had been homesick. They were very supportive, which helped. And Adam did a great job.

In school, I took as many required classes as I could. A bus transported all the students and our wheelchairs to different areas of the campus so we could arrive close to our classes. I had geology, Spanish, English composition, math, and the required physical education class. Thankfully, they allowed the physically handicapped students to use our PT to meet our physical education requirements. Once a day, I'd go to the gym, and PT students would do my normal range stretching therapy.

In class, I didn't have anyone write down notes for me, so I had to rely on my memory. Tests were often done at the library. I wore a headset and answered questions verbally through a microphone. This worked out well. Nearby students were often willing to help set everything up for me. Any homework I had I could do on my typewriter.

To stave off loneliness, I talked to my family once a week. I missed them a lot even though classes were going well, and I was happy with my decision to attend this school. It wasn't long, though, until I found a friend. Scott, another student on my dorm floor, was a lower level quadriplegic than me. He could move his arms quite a bit, but was somewhat limited in his finger movements. Scott was from Mississippi. We used to study together along with some of the other students. Every Monday night, we'd get together to watch Monday Night Football. Some guys would bring wine along, but I never cared for wine. I didn't mind having a couple of beers now and then, though. We enjoyed football. The University of Missouri Tigers had a good team and a bunch of us would go to the home football games together. I loved the camaraderie and the college celebration atmosphere of those sporting events. The spirit and enthusiasm was infectious. The band played, and cheerleaders got everyone involved. The adrenaline was pumping throughout the stadium. It was a wonderful experience—nothing else like it.

The only thing missing for me was a relationship. I still longed for a girlfriend—someone to share my thoughts and company with, someone who would need me like I needed her. Just feeling the presence, the touch, and perfume smell of a girlfriend was something I wanted to experience. Since Adam and I had many good conversations, he knew this. One day, we were on our way back to the dorm after he fed me at the cafeteria. He saw a couple of gals he knew and introduced me. Adam was engaged, so he did this for me. We exchanged the usual small talk and started talking about going to the football game that Saturday.

"Why don't you go the game with Randy?" Adam asked of one of the girls.

"I don't think so," she said kindly.

It was painful hearing that. No one likes rejection, even kind rejection. I'd be lying if I said it didn't hurt. I wondered what it was she didn't like. Was it me or the wheelchair? I knew the wheelchair made most people see me in a different light until they got to know me. But how could they get to know me if they couldn't look past the wheelchair? This was something with which I struggled.

After I had been at the university for over a month, Adam told me I had some red marks around my catheter at the spot where a metal urinal was in place at night to collect any urine that leaked out. After questioning him some more, he convinced me everything was okay. I knew sores of any kind could lead to major problems. I could feel they were there, but didn't feel pain. It concerned me because I'd seen fellow patients in the hospital who had pressure sores and had to be bedridden or even have surgery to help them heal. After another week, Adam said the sores had opened a bit. Now, I was really worried. When I talked to my parents that week, I told them. They decided to come down to check things out. I was happy to see them, but wished the circumstances were different. After seeing the sores, they decided I should see a doctor. The doctor didn't like the looks of them and said I needed to be bedridden for a few weeks for them to heal properly. Adam hadn't realized that a sore for me was much more serious than a sore for an able-bodied person. He felt bad, but it really wasn't his fault. Bed rest meant I had to leave the University of Missouri. I was sad to leave my new friends, but anxious to see my family and friends in Minnesota.

I loved being back home with my family. I cherished every moment with them because I knew it would be temporary. I was planning on going back to school for the winter semester. At home, the doctor said I'd need to be bedridden for six weeks to give the pressure sores time to heal. This was not welcome news. It was difficult to be restricted to my bed. I wanted the freedom to move about in my chair. Becky, Bob, and Linda were at school all day, Mom was at work, and Dad was working the farm. Since he no longer milked cows and now raised hogs and beef cattle along with doing crop farming, he had more flexibility to check on me. The fall harvest had just been completed. When Dad was busy during the day, a lady came to the house to do my daily cares and fix my meals. Without company and being confined to my bed, the days grew long. I wasn't a big TV watcher, so I did lots of reading and typing. Most often, I read sports biographies. I loved reading about the inspiring lives of sports heroes and the major role God played in their lives. I was also reading a beginner's version of the Bible. This heightened my hunger to know more about my God and to grow in my faith.

I enjoyed writing too. My typewriter was set up in front of me much like when Eric and I studied in the hospital. Even though I was bedridden, I was able to have my head up. With a table across my lap, I could either read or type with my mouthstick. My book was secured in a book holder. I didn't write stories, but did find myself writing down my thoughts. It was like keeping a journal and was very therapeutic. What I wrote depended on the day. It became an outlet, like confiding in a close friend. My typewriter became my secret way to vent. I could type as long as I wanted to since I had a long roll of paper that was fed into the typewriter. After I typed, the paper was torn off by someone in the family who placed it in the back of a dictionary my parents had given me when I left for college. I kept these writings very private. I wasn't willing to share that part of myself yet. My family respected that.

At the end of November, the long bed rest was drawing to a close. There was only another week or so until my sores would heal completely. I was excited knowing I'd soon be up and about, celebrating Christmas with my family and then heading back to the University of Missouri.

One day, Mr. Fisher stopped by the house. "I have some exciting news for you!" he said. "I'm pretty sure I can set things up for you to open your own telephone answering service in Austin." He was very excited about it. I wondered why now? Where was this idea coming from?

"How long would this take?" asked Mom.

"It'll take a while to set everything up, but I'm sure I can make it happen," said Mr. Fisher.

"I was planning on going back to the University of Missouri," I said.

"I think this would be a better route for you to take," he said.

While I appreciated the help vocational rehab was giving me, I never felt I had a voice in my future. The vocational rehab program helped provide my funding, so I didn't feel like I had a choice in the matter.

"I'll get back to you right after Christmas," Mr. Fisher said.

I didn't know how to feel. I was disappointed, but there was a small part of me that was excited about the chance to open my own business. The direction of my life had just made a complete turn, and I wasn't sure I liked it.

"What do you think about all this?" I asked Mom and Dad.

"Mr. Fisher thinks it would be best for you," said Dad.

"And you won't be far from home," added Mom.

I knew all of that was true, but I wasn't ready to accept it. I wanted a chance to make the choice for myself. I had just been through four months that involved homesickness, learning to be away from my family, developing strong friendships, and then having to return to bed rest. But I kept reminding myself that I wasn't in control—God was. He had already blessed me with some new friendships and experiences. I didn't know what was ahead for me, but I knew God was helping me grow and taking me on a journey. It was the uncertainty that didn't sit well. I had to learn that life wasn't always going to go as I had planned. I needed to be patient and see what would unfold.

Chapter 33
My Journey Continues

"Jesus replied, 'What is impossible
with men is possible with God'."
—Luke 18:27

By January 1973, I was anxiously waiting to hear back from my vocational rehab counselor. It was too late now to go back to college for the winter semester, so I was committed to do whatever Mr. Fisher developed. Soon, he called, apologizing to us for getting back to us later than expected.

"I have some leads on a couple locations for you to set up your answering service, Randy," he said. "Ideally, I want to find a place where you could live in the same place you have your business."

"What about an attendant to do my care needs?" I asked.

"I'm not concerned about that," he said. "I can always find someone through vocational rehab services."

"What kind of timeframe are we talking about?" asked Mom.

"That's my biggest obstacle right now," he said. "The people I need to talk to are leasing their buildings now. It could be some time before they become available. But I was thinking we could work out details in the meantime. We could get business cards made, find a phone with many lines that you could operate with your mouthstick, get a sign made, and any other details we could think of while we're waiting. What do you think about that?"

"Sounds okay to me," I said.

As Mr. Fisher was leaving, he said he'd get back to us when he knew more.

"What do you think about this idea?" Dad asked after Mr. Fisher left.

"In a way, it's kind of exciting, but I'm a little worried about how long it will take to get it started," I said.

"I was wondering the same thing," said Dad.

"We just have to keep in touch with Mr. Fisher to see how things are moving along," said Mom.

Overall, I still had mixed feelings about the answering service business. As weeks passed, and we heard nothing, my nervousness increased. I began wondering if it was even possible.

We made contact with Mr. Fisher from time to time, though, and he assured us things were progressing. That winter, we went to a lot of the Lyle high school home basketball games. It was a great distraction since I loved sports and the whole atmosphere. I knew many of the kids through Becky and because we were from a small town. Those games were refreshing, and I always left feeling good about things whether we won or lost.

Spring was approaching rapidly, though, and I felt so much time had been wasted. I could've finished the year at college. It was during this time that I really had to lean on God because I was frustrated. I missed my friends. I missed learning. The days were long. I prayed—prayer was the only place I received comfort. I sought God often and drew great peace from talking to Him.

Spring faded to summer, and I was thrilled to be outside again. Everything was going along well with my family. They were helpful with my care needs. I didn't read or write much in the summer. I just wanted to be outside. That summer, Jim, now twenty-two, got engaged to be married to a wonderful gal, Bonnie. She grew up on a farm a couple hours away, by the Mississippi River. She had family in the Austin area and moved here to attend Austin Junior College. Being a farm girl, she fit in perfectly with our family. I liked her from the beginning. I was happy for Jim and Bonnie! They set the date for August 1974. I still believed the time would come when I'd meet that special someone.

That summer, there was no news from my counselor. We finally met with him again in the fall. He assured me that I'd be living and working in my own apartment by the first part of 1974. We got business cards made with the business name, Randy's Telephone Answering Service; my name; my phone number; and the address. I couldn't wait to start working. After the sign was made, I got to meet the man from whom I'd be renting my apartment/business. He gave me a tour of the building, which would be set up so my business would be in the front and my apartment in the back. It was small, but I could see it working. Everything was set for me to open up in March. The business had a phone with several lines and a desk on which to put the phone, typewriter, and tape recorder.

When a call came in, I would answer the line that was blinking by pressing the button with my mouthstick. I recorded each message and typed it. I was confident I could make this happen. It seemed like the right fit.

All that was missing was an attendant to do my cares. Mr. Fisher found Bill, a young man just a couple years older than me who was slightly challenged mentally but had a big heart. He would also be my roommate. After Bill learned my cares, I was set to go. My parents and other family members supplied me with furniture for the apartment. I didn't need much since the apartment was small. The only way I could get inside it was through a back door that had no steps. We pulled the van up to the back door, lined up the portable ramps to the doorway, and then I wheeled inside. It certainly wasn't handy, but in those days, we had to make do. There was also a front entrance, but to use it, I had to go through the office of the business next to me. This was my landlord's business. I didn't like using this entrance because I felt it was bothersome. Soon, my business would open. For a year and a half, I had waited. I was ready.

CHAPTER 34
OPEN FOR BUSINESS

"For I know the plans I have for you,
declares the Lord, plans for welfare
and not for evil, to give you a future and a hope."
—Jeremiah 29:11

Randy's Telephone Answering Service did open, as promised, in March. After doing some advertising, I soon got my first clients. At the grand opening, the mayor of Austin was present for a ribbon cutting ceremony. This exposure also helped promote the business and gain customers. Family members were on hand that day too. They were really excited for me and supportive.

My attendant moved in with me immediately and did a good job with most of my cares. By now we had gotten a Hoyer lift. My body had grown into adulthood and it wasn't easy transferring me manually. The lift was a big help and operated on a simple premise. I was turned on my side, the sling tucked under me, and the lift was moved over my bed to attach the straps to the sling. The lift was then pumped up until I was in a sitting position, then it was maneuvered over my chair, and I was slowly lowered down onto my cushion. This procedure was reversed when transferring back to bed. Mom stopped by the apartment every morning on her way to work to do bowel care and ensure everything was going well. I took comfort in her presence, but felt guilty about having her check on me after I had moved away from home.

But she wasn't the only one who stopped by to check on me. Family members were frequent visitors. Jim and Bonnie stopped to chat about their upcoming August wedding. We were all very excited about it. Beck and her friends visited too. It was hard to believe she would graduate from high school in just over a month. When school got out for the summer, Bob and Linda came often and spent most of the day visiting. There was a hamburger joint half a block away, and sometimes they'd get hamburgers and French fries for us for dinner.

A curtain separated my office from the apartment. The office was barely big enough for my desk and wheelchair, but it worked and that's all that mattered. My apartment was very small too, but it served its purpose. It had been three months and business was starting to pick up as word got out. I was very busy by mid-June. At the initial consultation with the client, we determined when they needed their phones answered and how they wanted them answered. Usually, I answered phones over the dinner hour, after business hours, and on weekends. I had to pay close attention to which flashing light corresponded to which business line. I'd answer the call, take the message, type it out, and then relay it to the business owner. Every call was recorded, so I could always check back to ensure each detail was correct. I got quite adept at handling this job using my mouthstick. It felt good knowing I had a skill to put to use and that I could do something that made my family proud.

By summer, Beck had graduated and Jim's wedding was approaching. I didn't like being inside so often when the weather was nice, but that comes with the responsibility of work. But one thing I wouldn't miss out on was Jim's wedding. Mr. Fisher helped me find someone to answer phones. The wedding was beautiful! It wasn't terribly hot for an August day in Minnesota. Bonnie made her own dress, and it was gorgeous! My siblings were all involved in some capacity. As I watched the ceremony, I pictured my own wedding in my mind. Jim and Bonnie named me the honorary best man. Afterward, they moved into an apartment in Austin. Jim was now working at the Hormel meat packing factory and

Bonnie was going to school and working as a receptionist at a medical clinic.

The rest of the year passed quickly. Bob was a freshman, and Linda was a sixth grader. Becky started dating a nice man who went into the armed forces. I passed my free time going to Lyle high school basketball games. That meant, of course, that I had to find someone to answer the phones, but that worked fine since most of my work was done before I left for the games. In late November, the president of the Lyle Booster Club approached and asked, "Randy, would you be interested in being our public address announcer for all home sporting events?"

I was quite surprised, but answered, "Yeah, if it would work out in my schedule."

"Could you come Tuesday after school, and we could check everything out for you?" he asked.

"Yeah, I think that'll work. Thanks!"

I was really excited about this possibility! I told my parents about the opportunity, and they were thrilled. On Tuesday, Dad took me to the school. The industrial arts class had built a ramp so I could get up onto the stage. That was where all the announcing was done. We worked out a few quirks with the microphone stand, and it was clear everything would work out for me to begin serving as the announcer for all home Lyle athletic sporting events in December 1974. I was very familiar with sports. I knew the rules and the officials' hand signals. For basketball, I'd announce the playing of the national anthem, starting lineups, who made baskets, fouls, timeouts, substitutions, and everything else. It was the same for football, except there I had to announce the yardage gained on each play, the player or players involved in the play, the tackler, the down, the yards to go for a first down, any touchdowns, and then get ready for the next play. I felt comfortable in this role. Before every game I'd have the scorekeeper from the opposing team go through their roster. It was very important to me to have all the pronunciations down perfectly. I never wanted to mispronounce a player's name. I took this seriously. Sometimes, after a game, the opposing coach or a fan would come over to tell me how nice it was to have a PA announcer because few other schools in our area had one. I always appreciated this. Being the PA announcer helped me feel a part of the community. I had much for which to be thankful.

In early March, I began having problems with Bill. His social life was interfering with my cares. His friends came over to our small apartment at inappropriate times that interfered with his ability to do my cares. I tried the direct approach by having a long talk with him, but to no avail. Since my cares were critical to my health and comfort, this issue weighed heavily on my mind. One night, I turned to prayer. "God," I said, with a heavy heart, "you know my troubled heart better than I do. Help me make the decisions that are best for all of us. Help me make the right decisions about my future. Give me the answers as I sleep tonight. Thank you for your strength, peace, and love. I love you. Amen."

The next morning, I awoke with a clear picture of what I needed to do. Yes, I was having some problems with Bill, but the bigger issues were inside me. My business was doing well, and we were proud of it, but it had been wearing on me for some time. I knew I could handle the work, but it felt restrictive. With my office and apartment in the same place, I never got away from work. I was answering phones seven days a week. There was one particular stretch of time where I didn't leave my apartment for seven weeks! Aside from the telephone business and visits from my family, I never had contact with others. I felt a profound sense of isolation. This was not the lifestyle I wanted for the rest of my life. There was no joy in it.

Perhaps it was the sports announcer job that helped me see things more clearly. That job gave me a reason to leave my apartment and do something I enjoyed. In any case, I made up my mind that I wanted to end the telephone answering business. I had worked hard for over a year and knew in my heart it was time for me to move on to something else. I just didn't know how to tell everyone.

At that time, the family was getting ready for another wedding. Becky and Rick, her boyfriend, got engaged. They were planning to marry down the road, but the date had to be moved up as he was getting an unexpected leave from the military in April. They would marry that month so Beck could move to where he was stationed. Since the wedding was imminent, I decided to keep my thoughts inside until after her marriage. I didn't want to ruin the celebration.

After the wedding, Becky and Rick moved near Chicago, where he was stationed. It was hard having a family member move away, but I was happy for them. I was only twenty-one-years-old and still knew I'd get married someday.

I knew I couldn't prolong telling the family about my decision any longer. I prayed for the right words to say and the strength to do it. Even though what I was about to do was one of the most difficult things I'd ever had to do, I knew in my heart it was the right decision. So, one day, I told my parents I needed to talk to them. As most children feel, I wanted to make them proud and not disappoint them. I worried I was about to do the opposite. Mom and Dad came to my place, and I opened my heart to them.

"Are you sure about this?" Dad asked.

"Yeah, I'm very sure," I said.

"Now, what will you do?" he asked.

"I'd like to take the broadcasting course at the Austin Vocational Technical School," I said.

Mom didn't say much. She just listened. While Dad never said he was disappointed with my decision, I sensed that he was, and it hurt. Work was very important to Dad. He thought hard work and dedication showed the character of a man. I happened to agree. I felt terrible, and I told them that.

"Randy," said Mom. "We'll get through this."

I appreciated her kindness with her standard comforting remark.

"You'll need to contact everyone and tell them," said Dad.

I promised I would. They left, and I felt empty. Still, I proceeded with my decision, even though it was hard. I began contacting my vocational rehab counselor and customers to tell them Randy's Telephone Answering Service was closing. It was a very difficult time. I'd never been a quitter, and I hoped people didn't perceive me that way. I knew God wanted me to be happy. I'd learned life isn't about making the popular decision; it's about making the right one. And I knew this was right.

Chapter 35
Broadcasting School

"The steps of a man are established by the Lord, when he delights in his way."
—Psalm 37:23

When the business closed, there was nowhere to go but back home. I moved back in July 1975. It seemed strange living there without Jim and Becky, but it was still home. Bob and Linda helped Mom and Dad with my cares. It was wonderful to be there, not alone, surrounded by people I cared about. Still, I knew I had decisions to make soon about my future. I prayed for guidance, and I took action. The first thing I did was contact Mr. Fisher about my intentions to take the Radio/TV Communications course at the Austin Vocational Technical Institute. He said he'd check on the course. The next day, he called to tell me there were a couple openings, but the instructor wanted to meet me to see if it would be feasible for me to take the course. Mr. Fisher, my parents, and I met with him the following week.

"So, you'd like to take this course, huh?" asked Mr. Sam Howard.

"Yeah, I really would."

"Would it work for you to come in tomorrow for a couple of hours and observe what goes on here?" he asked.

"That shouldn't be a problem," I answered.

"I can drop him off and pick him up a few hours later," offered Dad.

On the way home, Mom said she liked the instructor. She thought he seemed kind.

"I remember seeing him on the news when I was a kid," I said, impressed.

"He worked in radio too," said Dad.

Mr. Howard was a community celebrity, a real personality. He was a big man with a booming voice. He certainly seemed intimidating, but there was also something endearing about him. He seemed to be caring and a gentle soul.

The next day, Dad dropped me off at the broadcasting course. Mr. Howard, or Sam as he preferred to be called, explained to the students why I was there. The class I was observing was part of a twelve month course that would be ending in a week. The next class would start in two weeks. The room held two radio booths in the main section. Each was cut in half. On one half was the disc jockey. A newsperson was in the other half. A window divided the rooms so the DJ could give the newsperson hand cues. The TV studio was located at the other end of the building. It was also the site of Austin's public television studio. After he showed me the layout, Sam let me look around a bit longer and then had me come into his office.

"So, what do you think?" he asked.

"It really looks interesting! I'd love to take this course," I said.

"Just from what I've seen of you today, I think it would be a good fit for both of us. How about I talk to your counselor, get you signed up, and you can start the course in two weeks?"

"Sounds great!" I said, unable to contain my smile.

Dad came after to take me home. On the way, I told him about the experience. I'd always had a big interest in broadcasting. It started when Dad and I used to listen to baseball games on the radio. There was excitement in the air. A good announcer could make you feel like you were right in on the action. I was physically limited after my accident, but I could still talk fine. If my broadcasting skills were honed, this would only improve my chances of future employment. When I was doing the PA announcing, my personality completely changed. I felt outgoing and free behind the microphone and enjoyed this renewed change. I felt this course would only improve my skills. I couldn't wait to learn more about it.

When it was time for school to begin, I was ready to go. My broadcasting class had thirty students of varying ages—from those just out of high school to some students well into their thirties. Our instructor welcomed us all and then said, pointing at me, "As you can all see, we have a young man in a wheelchair in our class. I'm sure he'd appreciate you opening the door for him and any other bits of help you could offer him when you see it's needed."

This was all he ever said about my wheelchair. After he said it, I felt all eyes on me. But, from that moment on, I was treated as just another classmate. I had found my niche. I was fitting in and loved it. The thirty of us had such different personalities, but we all meshed nicely. The darkness I had buried deep within me in junior and senior high school was now being lifted. The moment I started to just be myself was liberating. The pain and hurt was no longer inside. I was blessed to be a student in this class. God had set me free!

The first few weeks of class were spent learning the duties that needed to be done during a day in radio and TV, such as writing commercials, filling out a daily report of the shift details, preparing news reports and sports reports, and much more. Each day, we were each assigned a certain duty. One day, you might be the DJ. The next, you could be the newsperson, the commercial writer, the person who put the shift report together, or one of the TV workers. Some duties took a lot of time and others not much. From one day to the next, you could either be very busy or have lots of down time. We had the freedom to come and go as long as our work got done. There was a great deal of time spent in the student commons, which allowed us to bond as classmates and people. Over time, we talked more about our backgrounds and grew quite close. I was thrilled to be part of the group. This was the first time I'd been in a social atmosphere since grade school and my brief experience at the University of Missouri.

Back in Lyle, I still did the PA announcing whenever there was a home game. At home, Becky had returned from Hawaii, where her husband was stationed. She was on an extended visit since Rick was at sea for six months. It was great to see her again and spend time with her. She wanted to hear all about my broadcasting class, and, one day, she asked, "Could I come and visit at school?" Since my instructor didn't have any problems with it, Becky did. Our class atmosphere was informal, so she stopped by often and became good friends with my classmates. One of my best friends was a gal, Joan, who lived about three hours from Austin. We had a great deal in common. She too was from a small town and had lived on a farm. Family and spirituality was very important to Joan, and we shared many of the same values. She and Becky also became good friends. Joan didn't always go home on the weekends because it was so far away, so she'd come out to the farm instead. We loved having her there.

One day, Beck and I were talking about her, and I said, "I'm thinking about asking Joan on a date. What do you think of that?"

"You guys are such good friends," said Beck. "I hope it wouldn't ruin that."

This wasn't the response I wanted, but I understood where Beck was coming from. "Yeah, you're probably right," I said.

I decided not to pursue it any further. I regretted this decision, but I realized God was taking Joan down the path He had planned for her. He would do the same for me. For a while, I wished I had asked her out, but I got to see her every day in class. This eased the hurt, and time healed it. Why wallow in what might have been? Besides, friendships aren't always easy to come by, and ours was special. I shared the darkness I had buried within me with her one day in the student commons. She simply sad, "Randy, we all love you!" I thanked God for Joan.

The social scene and parties with my newfound friends kept me distracted from my feelings. Beck took me to a lot of parties. I drank too much alcohol, usually beer, and I even tried smoking marijuana a few times. I was not skilled at this since my respiratory system is limited and I have less lung capacity due to my paralysis. I couldn't inhale enough to experience the effects, and so I didn't continue. I did drink too much at the time, and it clouded my thinking, affecting the priorities in my life. In fact, I was thinking so much about my social life that I had less and less time for God. I either never realized it or refused to acknowledge it. Drinking was an escape. I felt my worries and concerns left when I partied. I was with friends who didn't judge me. They accepted me for who I was. We talked about music, our families, and the future. I couldn't wait for the next weekend, the next party. I soon realized I was so wrong! I started feeling the emptiness inside when I wasn't partying. I missed God in my life. I had put God second by simply not focusing on Him. I've messed up many times in my life. I fall short at times, but when all is said and done, I know God forgives me. I try to learn each time I fall short.

Class was also a welcome distraction. And I had so much fun that year. Once, we taped a skit for TV and the script turned out to be about a humorous situation for each of us. When it was my turn to speak, my line was, "I can't believe I got a ticket for jaywalking!" The student who was on cue after me started to snicker. Soon, the whole crew was laughing. The laugh started slowly and grew to a deep belly laugh that we couldn't stop. Even our instructor was laughing. Needless to say, the taping stopped.

Toward the end of the year, when we had one month left, Joan and I were in the student commons, and she said to me, "Just think, in a month we'll be done with school and go our separate ways. Randy, I promise to always stay in touch with you. Do you promise to always stay in touch with me?"

"I promise," I said.

After school, she got a job closer to her hometown, so it wasn't possible to see each other, but true to her word, she did write, and so did I. She'd update me on her career and activities, and once she wrote to tell me about a man she met. Later, she wrote to tell me they were engaged. While I was happy for her, I also felt a pang of regret. I have to admit, I was jealous of her fiancé. She was incredibly special. I hoped that our friendship wouldn't suffer after she married. In the end, I was glad she found someone she loved. She deserved the best. Joan invited my entire family to her wedding. We were thrilled to be part of her day. It was at the wedding that I got to meet Chris, her fiancé, now husband. They seemed well suited. I could tell they'd make a great couple and hoped they'd be blessed with a wonderful family.

In late summer 1976, I received my FCC license and graduated with a degree in broadcasting. I had chosen this path, and I had completed the studies. The class had been rewarding for me. It was a way to have a say in my own destiny, to pursue what I believed God wanted me to do. At this time, I contacted vocational rehab services to tell them I wouldn't need their assistance any longer. I felt I was fully capable of making my own decisions concerning my future.

My decision was confirmed when I was chosen as one of four in my class to announce the names of the graduates at commencement. It was a true honor. After graduation, and I got my priorities set by putting my main focus on God again. He returned to the number one spot in my life. I felt I had grown so much!

CHAPTER 36
WHERE TO NOW, GOD?

"Bear one another's burdens, and
so fulfill the law of Christ."
—Galatians 6:2

By fall of 1976, it had been over ten years since I broke my neck. Jim and Bonnie were still living in their Austin apartment, Beck was back in Hawaii, Bob was sixteen and would be a junior, and Linda was thirteen and headed into eighth grade. My family had grown so much, and they had grown into wonderful people. Bob was already planning on attending electronics school, Jim was working at Hormel, Bonnie was starting nursing school, and Becky was working at a convenience store. I too wanted a vocation. This was weighing on my mind. The unknown is many times the worst to deal with.

I was trying to decide what to do with my life when an opportunity arose for me at the Austin Voluntary Action Center (VAC), a cause that was near and dear to my heart because it got volunteers involved with helping people have their essential needs met. Some needs were elderly and handicapped individuals getting transportation to medical appointments, getting groceries, having pets find temporary homes, and so many more daily activities. People would call the VAC with their needs and the VAC did the rest.

The idea of working there excited me. I accepted the job as communications coordinator, which entailed finding out what the weekly needs were by being in daily contact with the VAC. After talking with the VAC coordinator, I'd type up a report and tape it in the TV studio at Austin Vocational Technical School. Then, the tape was sent to the two radio stations in Austin to be aired at various times throughout the week.

Here was a job that fulfilled me. It gave me a sense of accomplishment, and I felt like I was making a difference—helping other people's needs be met by spreading the word. It was heartwarming to find so many willing volunteers. It made me appreciate my family even more. They had always been there for me!

Of course, I was my biggest critic. No matter how much I'd trained for this, I found it difficult to listen to myself on the radio. I always thought I could do better and tried to do so the next time. The radio officials from both stations were always pleased with my reports and the quality of the announcing. We developed a good working relationship. It amazed me how many people heard those reports. Folks came up to me when they saw me to tell me how much they enjoyed them. I never felt comfortable receiving compliments, but I knew I was blessed to be doing what I loved.

At this time, I continued my PA announcing and was also speaking publicly to groups about handicapped awareness. I was invited to speak at schools, clubs, and other organizations. I told my story and explained that, with the exception of sitting in a wheelchair, I'm just like anyone else. At the end of my presentation, I held a question and answer period. I loved it! With the sincerity and honesty of kids, they brought all their questions to the table. I answered very openly and tried to never cover anything up. I also talked about how faith helped me on my journey. When I talked with older audiences, I explained how judging and labeling others is dangerous. I shared many thoughts with them. I told them what my heart felt. Some people say it's merely offering an opinion, but when you form a belief about someone else without knowing him or his situation, it's just judgment. We all experience it at one time or another. I know I did. It hurts. I'm still Randy. We all have emotions and strengths and weaknesses. People have their own abilities, no matter what their limitations. People are quick to judge. We've all done it. Our tongues are the sharpest weapon we possess. Words cut deeply. Labeling and judging is hurtful to others and to ourselves. It keeps us from reaching out to others who may need us. It keeps us from being the best we can be.

Over the years, the laws changed things completely. Now, all public places need to be handicapped accessible. What a different world from the 1960s! I wake up in the morning, get in my wheelchair, and can pretty much go anywhere I want with my modified van. Now, I no longer think about accepting things and adjusting to them. I just go and live life.

I couldn't thank the Lord enough for these opportunities. I turned to him more and more as my partner in this journey. One day, I was thinking about this, and, with tears of joy in my eyes, I prayed, "God, you are always so good to me! I want you to know how much I appreciate your blessings. Please continue to give me your strength to reach out to others. I promise to always do your will. I love you so much. Amen!"

The year was going by fast, and soon it would be spring. I helped out on the farm as much as possible, including keeping track of corn and soybean prices and passing them on to Dad. Mom asked me to make sure Bob and Linda got their homework done. Linda started the meal, and Bob did his chores, but I never had to remind them what to do because they were very responsible.

The fall of 1977, Eric, my First East roommate, got married. He and Ann, his fiancée, asked me to be their best man. Eric was still in a wheelchair because of polio, and doing fine. He had graduated from Southwest State University with a history degree. That's where he met Ann. They both were from a town just west of Austin, only thirty miles away. Their wedding was in their hometown, and I was thrilled to be part of it. Like Jim and Beck's, it was a beautiful wedding. This was the third wedding of someone close to me I had witnessed. Instead of thinking my day would come, I now wondered *if* it would come. This was another concern. I gave it to God. I prayed, "God, help me follow your plan and be happy with the journey you have ahead for me. I love you. Amen!"

I'd stayed in touch with Eric and his family since we met in 1966. We remained very close, like brothers. A few months could go by without our being in touch, but when we connected again, it was as if we saw each other recently. Years later, when they had their first child, a boy, I was asked to be one of his godparents.

Overall, everything was going well in my life. If there was one thing I wished to change, it was to be more independent. I wanted a place of my own to live. There was an eight unit apartment building in Lyle that was just a few years old. I put my name on the waiting list for an apartment. I knew it might be a long wait.

Another year passed. Perhaps it was just my growing older, but time seemed to grow wings. Bob was graduating this year. He'd signed up for a two year course in electronics at the Austin Vocational Technical School. Linda couldn't wait for her sophomore year to start because she knew she'd be playing varsity volleyball and basketball. I was honored and proud to announce her name at the games. Again, time flew by.

By 1980, Becky and her husband had moved back from Hawaii, Jim and his wife were expecting their first child, Bob had graduated from the electronics class, and Linda was a senior. My parents were doing fine. It was then that I received a phone call informing me there was an apartment available. Life was going well. I was looking forward to the next phase.

CHAPTER 37
NEW OPPORTUNITIES

"Be glad in the Lord, and rejoice, O righteous,
and shout for joy all you upright in heart."
—Psalm 32:11

Everything had been progressing smoothly for the past three years, but changes were coming. The apartment turned out to be handicapped accessible. It wasn't very big, but it met my needs. It had two bedrooms, which was perfect because my night attendant could use the spare bedroom. Mom couldn't do any of my cares for a while. Recently, she'd had carpal tunnel surgery on her wrists. The repetitive work she had done for years at the Hormel plant caused the damage. Instead, we found Lois, a lady from Lyle, who was hired by the state as a personal care assistant (PCA).

On July 1, 1980, I moved into the apartment. Three young men from the high school worked for me at night doing my cares: transferring me from my wheelchair to the bed, handling my catheter care, turning and positioning me in the night, and anything else I needed. They each worked about ten nights a month. This was before the state required them to be eighteen. Since they used the spare bedroom, I could easily awaken them if I needed something. Lois, my PCA, came at various times throughout the day to do my cares.

Working at my desk (1980)

Uncle Bob built a desk for me that I could access with my motorized wheelchair. My brother Bob, who is named after my uncle, modified it for me over the years. Once I pull up to my desk, I can grab my mouthstick with my mouth and then do a number of things with it, like turning on my remotes for the TV, the overhead kitchen light, or stereo; calling someone on my speaker telephone by pushing the buttons; answering the phone by pushing the speaker button; turning on the desk lamp by placing the mouthstick through a circular loop attached to the lamp and pulling down; operating my computer by pressing the keyboard buttons; and more. I feel like I can do anything! And I'm still using the same mouthstick piece that was designed for me in OT in 1966. My mouthstick has a hard plastic piece that is formed to the size of my mouth. The middle is cut out so I can talk even with the mouthstick in my mouth. Attached to the plastic mouthpiece is a wooden stick about a foot long. At the end of it is a rubber tip, which allows me to turn pages in a book. Today, there are voice activated gadgets that would allow me to do all of this at a much faster pace, but

I'm not a big fan of change. My mouthstick works just fine. This allows me to live a very independent lifestyle. I loved my apartment, and the freedom I now had!

The month after I moved in, Jim and his wife had a baby boy. They named him Jimmy, after his dad. It was wonderful being an uncle, and I was thrilled when they asked me to be one of his godparents! About the same time, Becky told us she was expecting and due in February. Soon, I would have two nephews! Our family was growing.

Professionally, changes where coming. I was still doing PA announcing and spreading awareness about the physically handicapped, but in the spring of 1981, the VAC closed because there wasn't enough funding. It was a job I had loved. Uncertainty set in, but I held on to faith. I knew God would open another door. God had blessed me deeply. I thanked Him for my two nephews, my wonderful family, the opportunity to live independently in my apartment, the opportunity to work for the VAC, and the many daily blessings. I knew He had another plan in store for me, and I couldn't wait to see what it was.

Late in the summer of 1981, I was pondering what to do. Just sitting in my apartment wasn't an option. The Lyle school kept popping in my head. By now, I realized God was talking to me. I couldn't ignore him, so I talked with the Lyle school superintendent. He told me they were always in need of volunteers. I immediately volunteered. This is one of the best decisions I ever made! I had a strong connection with the school district since I'd been doing the announcing for nearly six years. I loved working with kids. I thought this would be a natural fit. They opened their arms to me, and I was very excited to begin this new venture. My role was to assist in the learning disabilities (LD) department, with the Title 1 program, summer school programs, and eventually, helping teach kids some computer basics. In the end, those kids taught me more than I could ever teach them. And I grew in my faith.

In the Title 1 program, I quickly discovered that the lead teacher and another aide were Christians. We shared our love for the Lord. I loved the Lord, but I was still feeling a bit of struggle, an emptiness.

I wanted to fill that void. In 1982, Karen, the lead teacher in Title 1, asked me to meet her husband, Dennis. They came by the apartment to visit a few times. One night, I told them about the emptiness I felt.

"Would you like to pray about it?" asked Dennis.

"Yes, I would," I said.

"Dear heavenly Father, we ask you fill Randy's heart with your love and peace as only you can do. Fill the emptiness he feels inside," he prayed.

"God, I can't do this by myself! I ask Jesus to come into my heart and make me complete! In the name of Jesus, I pray, amen!" I added.

Though I was already a Christian, I had just recommitted my life to the Lord. I felt a sense of completeness. It wasn't an earth shattering event. It was part of a process. It was part of my story, part of how I came to the Lord. This reawakening enlivened my relationships with others too. I found camaraderie and lifelong friendships with many in the Lyle elementary school. One such friendship was with Cindy, the elementary LD teacher and summer school coordinator. She was the best teacher I had ever met! We became close friends and still are today. We too share a love for the Lord.

I also found laughter. There's nothing quite like the sound of it. Laughter is so uplifting, and it fills your heart with joy. I knew God wanted us to be joyful. And the more I experienced life, the more I grew convinced that He has a wonderful sense of humor!

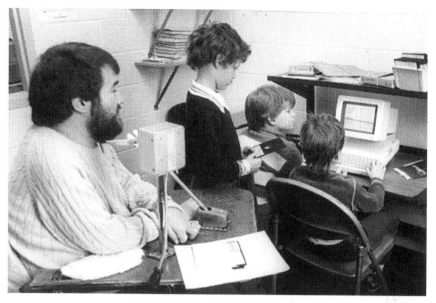

Teaching computers (1984)

One day, after I'd been in the school for a number of years, I was teaching computers to third graders. One of them looked at me for a second and said, "So, you can't move, huh?"

"No," I said. "I hurt my neck a long time ago, and, because of that injury, I can't move my arms or legs."

"Maybe you just aren't trying hard enough!" he said quickly.

Before I could say anything, one of the other kids chimed in, "He's paralyzed and can't move, okay?"

That seemed to clarify things for the boy who asked. Ironically, the boy in question was not known to be motivated. He had probably heard that phrase from his parents and teachers many times. I wore a smile on my face the rest of the day.

Another time, I was at a softball game, watching my brothers play, and a little boy, about four years old, asked, "Do you have a broken leg?"

"No, I broke my neck and can't move my arms or legs," I said.

He stared for a couple of seconds and asked, "Then, why is your head still on?"

Though I felt like bursting out laughing, I managed to stay composed and said, "My neck was hurt on the inside, and that's why I can't move."

Satisfied, he went on his way. Kids are amazing individuals, and their presence is uplifting. It made perfect sense to that boy. You break your neck, and the head should fall off. Jesus always had a soft spot in his heart for children, and understandably so. Their honesty and sincerity is refreshing.

Humor helped me keep things in perspective. In addition to the fun and inspiration I gained from working with the children, I also looked to my dad for comic relief. He loved to tell stories and jokes. He just had a special knack for it. Even if the joke wasn't funny, somehow he made you laugh. I was terrible at joke telling, so I admired his gift. He could always make you feel better inside.

The rest of my family was another source of joy. We loved to laugh, which made us closer. At family gatherings, after the meal, I sometimes said, "I nominate all the men do the dishes today!" The women rapidly agreed with me, but I got a few dirty looks from the guys. Once, Linda and I were in the kitchen and there happened to be a chocolate cream pie on the counter. She picked it up and, trying to be funny, faked liked she was going to throw it in my face. But it started to slip. In an effort to gain control of it, she pushed the pie against the side of my face. I was shocked to say the least. She fell to the floor, rolling in laughter. Neither of us could stop laughing. The whole left side of my face was covered with chocolate cream pie. It was stuck in my ear and hair. Mom came out and asked, "What happened?" We tried to answer, but couldn't. Mom started laughing too. Eventually, we got our laughter under control, and they cleaned me up. It wasn't easy cleaning chocolate pie out of my ear.

Sometimes, when we were all together, I'd sit back and listen to the sounds. I loved listening to Becky's laughter. It was infectious. And I never knew what Linda's husband, Randy, was up to next. Even though we shared the same name, he was usually referred to as Linda's Randy.

He fit in nicely with our family since he was quite a jokester. Whenever he walked by me, he tried to inconspicuously turn my chair off. Then, he'd laugh when I tried moving but had no power. I soon got wise to his ways.

A lot happened around the dining room table too. Once, Linda's Randy and Becky were in the kitchen. Linda was eating some chips, and she hollered to her husband, "Bring in the dip, will you?" Next thing we saw was Randy carrying Becky into the dining room.

"What are you doing?" asked Linda.

"You said, 'Bring in the dip!'" he responded.

We all got a good laugh out of that. Becky included.

Certainly, I'd gone through many challenges in my life and, when I think back on them, it was laughter that helped get me through. My family provided so much of it, but even during the grueling and lonely times on First East, laughter filled the halls every evening. I learned to never take myself too seriously. If the laughter couldn't get through the dark times, I knew I'd never see the light.

CHAPTER **38**
FAMILY TRAGEDIES

"Blessed are those who mourn,
for they will be comforted."
—Matthew 5:4

Mom and Dad (1985)

By 1985, there had been many changes in my family. Mom was on disability retirement because her hands were worn out after working for thirty-seven years at the Hormel factory. She'd had multiple carpal tunnel surgeries and even a joint replacement in her thumb, but to no avail. She was now limited in her abilities. This was hard on her. She'd loved painting and doing crafts, but couldn't do what she once had. Dad wasn't doing well either. He'd been having uncomfortable feelings in his upper chest and throat area for some time. A number of doctor's visits couldn't produce a diagnosis. Thankfully, Jim was nearby to help out. He and his family had moved to a small farm just down the road from Mom and Dad.

Becky was having her own struggles. She'd gotten a divorce and was living in Austin with her son, Kory. We'd all begun to notice her mood swings. She wasn't the happy-go-lucky person she used to be. A few years later, she was diagnosed with bipolar disorder and manic depression, a diagnosis that would haunt her for years to come.

By January 1987, we thought we had some answers on Dad's condition. The doctors decided to remove his gallbladder in hopes it would alleviate some of the pain he had in his stomach and throat. After the surgery, he wasn't recovering like he should. As time went on, he decided to go to Mayo Clinic for further testing. He was hospitalized at St. Marys, but they couldn't find anything wrong with him. Our family was frustrated. The doctors wanted the family to convince Dad to go to their stress unit. We thought the doctors knew best, so we talked Dad into trying it. I can still see the tears in his sad eyes as we talked. Reluctantly, he agreed to go. It was a painful experience to have to do this, and to watch our strong father in his moment of weakness. I asked God to grant Dad peace and healing in his mind and body.

The next day, Dad called Mom and asked her to come and get him. He couldn't stand being there. Mom did. When I heard this, I was disappointed Dad didn't stay to get help. One day, when I was visiting at the farm, I sat at my parents' dining room table with Mom and Bob. Bob had graduated with a degree in electronics and was working in Rochester but living near the farm on an acreage he bought. That day I looked out the window, watching Dad slowly walk across the yard.

"Something is wrong with Dad," I said. "He's not himself. It almost looks like he's slowly dying."

Both Mom and Bob agreed with me. We felt helpless and didn't know what more we could do. He wasn't well. About two weeks later, on a Sunday night, Dad called on Bob to take him to the Austin emergency room. Dad was admitted to the hospital and got more testing. We prayed this would help.

The following Wednesday morning, Joyce, a different attendant, arrived at 4:00 a.m.

"Why are you here so early?" I asked.

"Your Mom called," she said. "The doctor wants your family to go to the hospital because your Dad isn't doing well."

My heart sank. Joyce got me ready and took me to the hospital, with her husband following behind in their vehicle. On the way, I prayed, "God, please let Dad be okay." But I knew this wasn't good or they never would've called the family together. When the van pulled up to the hospital, Linda met us. She was crying.

"Randy, he's gone," she said.

"I didn't make it in time!" I said, sobbing.

"It wouldn't have mattered," Linda reassured me. "They wouldn't let any of us in to see him."

Dad passed away on March 11, 1987, at the age of sixty-two, four months before Mom and Dad's fortieth wedding anniversary. Mom was a widow at fifty-nine. My heart ached for her. I never wished that my arms could move more than at that moment. I wanted to hug her. I wanted to comfort her. And I couldn't. I couldn't even make sense of any of it. Dad's death, the loss, and the pain of our family members hurt so badly. Dad was sick, but I never thought he would die. I never thought of the world without him. And here it was. The world kept turning regardless. I wanted to shout, "Stop! My dad just died!" But life went on.

The doctor asked Mom if it would be okay to do an autopsy. She agreed. The autopsy showed Dad had an ulcer on his esophagus. It eventually ate a hole in his aorta, causing him to bleed to death. The doctor said Dad had been suffering from this condition for twenty years.

After Dad's death, the circle of life continued. In June 1988, Linda had a baby boy, Mathew. When she found out she was pregnant, she told me, "Randy, Dad will never see my kids."

"He'll see them, all right," I reassured her. "He'll be their guardian angel."

She nodded, tears in her eyes.

In 1990, Mom sold the farm and bought a small house in Lyle. The family continued growing. Linda gave birth to another boy, Ray, in December 1991, and a girl in January 1994, Jessica. Jim and Bonnie had a little girl, Kim, in March 1995. And in May, Bob got married at the age of thirty-five. He'd once told me, "I'm not getting married for the sake of being married. It's got to be the right one." I respected that. The woman he married, Dar, is a wonderful woman who was divorced. She had a thirteen-year-old daughter, Staci. I had gained a sister-in-law and a beautiful niece with Bob's marriage. And I was honored to be their best man. Staci was the maid of honor.

In 1997, I retired from PA announcing. It was getting more and more difficult to go out and about in the cold Minnesota winters for the basketball games. There was also some decline in high school sportsmanship. The innocence of it was fading away. Things had changed so much from when I started. While I'd enjoyed announcing for twenty-two years, it had begun to lose its luster, and I was ready for a break.

In May 1999, I met a lady who had moved into my apartment building. Mary was divorced and a couple of years younger than me. We became good friends and started dating in late summer. My family liked her and always invited her to family gatherings. We got along great and had a spiritual connection. I was happy to be in a relationship, my first, and we truly cared about one another. Mary and I would go out to eat, meet with friends, and mostly talk. From the start, we spoke openly about my physical limitations. This was never an issue for her, and I appreciated that. I always had concerns this would be a potential problem. My concerns turned out to be unfounded. We were intimate to a degree, but it wasn't the basis to our relationship. I thanked God for this opportunity, one I prayed for my entire adult life.

As the months went on, I'd sometimes awaken in the middle of the night, wondering what I'd gotten myself into. I tried to ignore the feeling, but it kept recurring. By winter, I knew the relationship was wrong. It didn't feel right. I cared very much for Mary and enjoyed her companionship. But I soon learned some of the things she told me were less than truthful. I found out from a friend of hers that she'd lied about her past and family. Sometimes I'd catch the lies when she retold stories. She couldn't keep her untruthfulness straight. I didn't care about her background, but I cared about honesty. I lost trust. I knew I couldn't be in a relationship where truth and honesty were not the foundation. I asked God for the strength to get through it and to end the relationship.

Later, it became clear to me that the feelings I had were God's way of talking to me. I realized I wasn't truly in love with Mary. Instead, I was in love with the idea of being in love. This was unfair to both of us. I needed to end the relationship, but I knew it would hurt her. One day in spring of 2000, she came down and sat on my couch. I looked at her and said honestly and as gently as I could, "Our relationship just isn't going to work. We need to end it. I'm so sorry."

She started crying, got up, and left. I tried consoling her as she left, but I'm sure they sounded like empty words. A short time later, she moved. I never saw her again. I don't regret our relationship. It was a great experience. But I hated knowing I had hurt her. I felt empty inside again, despite knowing I was making the right decision. The relationship lasted one year.

That summer of 2000 was filled with reconnecting with friends and family. They had taken a backseat to my relationship with Mary. That's the way a relationship works, and I was okay with that. I helped with Vacation Bible School. I was ready for school to start.

I worked in the Lyle elementary school for one more year, but I retired from there in the fall of 2001 due to some health issues. I was having terrible sweating spells on just the right side of my face, neck, and shoulder. After my visit to Mayo, they decided it was caused from ruptured vertebrae in my lower back from many years in the wheelchair. The pain manifested itself with the sweating episodes. They took so much out of me and left me exhausted. They couldn't operate and hoped the problems would subside. After a few months they lessened some. With different wheelchairs, I've been able to redistribute my weight. Now I only have periodic clamminess. These health issues led to my retirement from school in 2001. Working at school was the best twenty years of my life, and I missed it so much. I had loved working with the kids. They had given more to me than I could ever give them.

Family continued to give me solace, strength, and enjoyment. But tragedy struck again on April 17, 2004. We were having a birthday party for Jim's daughter, Kimmy, and Linda's two youngest, Ray and Jessica. Kimmy's birthday was in March, and we always celebrated Ray and Jessie's birthdays around this time to give them a celebration separate from their actual Christmastime birthdays. The day was gorgeous, with temperatures in the 70s and bright sunshine. The party was at Mom's place, and the whole family was there, with the exception of Becky, who continued having struggles with mental illness. By now, she had stopped coming to most family gatherings. But everyone else was there, except for Linda and her daughter, Jessie. Linda had to work until noon that day. Randy brought the two boys. Jessie wanted to wait and come with her mom. They were late, and Randy, said, "I wonder where Linda and Jessie are? They should've been here by now."

Shortly after, the phone rang. We could hear Mom say, "Linda calm down—I can't understand you!"

Randy grabbed the phone quickly and asked, "Linda, what's wrong?"

"Jessie can't breathe!" he shouted as he dropped the phone and ran out the door. Bonnie, an RN, and Staci rushed out the door with him. It felt like the air was sucked out of Mom's house as they left. As it turned out, Linda and Jessie had been in a car accident five miles from Mom's. Staci sped them to the accident sight. Jessie was airlifted to St. Marys emergency room in Rochester. Bob took Linda's boys home with him to Rochester. Linda was taken to the Austin Emergency Room for treatment on her knee and foot, but refused to stay. She had a badly sprained knee and ligament damage to her foot. She signed release papers, and Randy's sister drove Linda to Rochester.

It was hard to wait at Mom's for news. But we kept getting phone call updates. We knew she was hurt badly and had broken bones and damage to some internal organs. She was in bad shape, but I figured she'd go through a long rehab process, like I did, and be okay. During the night, the doctors tried taking her off of life support to see if she would respond, but she didn't. By the next morning, we knew she had extensive brain damage and a slim chance of survival. They would try taking her off life support that afternoon at 2:00 p.m.

Jimmy, Jim's son, drove Mom and me to the hospital. All our family members were there. We took turns saying good-bye to Jessie. When it was my turn, I wheeled up to her bed, and Bonnie took my hand and placed it on Jessie's. When I said good-bye, it meant so much to have my hand touching Jessie's hand. Being able to touch her allowed me to feel a special connection. I'll never forget it.

"Jessie," I said. "I love you so much! Now, you'll be in the loving arms of Jesus!"

Everyone was crying, even the doctors and nurses. How does anyone make sense of the meaningless death of a beautiful, vibrant ten-year-old girl? Jessie was pronounced dead on April 18, 2004, after they removed life support. As I sobbed, our pastor came over to me and, rubbing my back, said, "It's a broken world we live in, isn't it?"

All I could do was nod my head in agreement. Linda and Randy made the painful and beautiful decision to donate Jessie's organs. That night, just as when Dad died, I couldn't sleep. I kept hearing a certain phrase about the angels singing and the white doves flying. God was giving me the words to a poem for Jessie, which I read at her funeral:

My favorite picture of Jessie (1999)

We Love You, Dear, Sweet Jessie
Dear Jess,
The angels are singing, and the white doves fly.
It's time to say good-bye,
But only for a while.
For when our time here is up, we'll come
join you and again see your Smile.

We hurt inside, and our hearts ache.
Sense of this, we cannot make.

Your life with us was way too short.
We have mixed feelings we are trying to sort.

Jess, your family and friends love you so much;
So many lives you did touch.

Grandpa Krulish you've finally met.

You're playing with him, I'm willing to bet.

I know you are looking down on us.
I can almost feel your soft, sweet touch.

Oh, the angels sing, and the white doves fly,
It's time to say good-bye,
But only for a while.
For when our time here is up, we'll come
join you and again see your Smile.

We know you're in a better place.
When I close my eyes, I see your face.

Everywhere I look, there you are.
I see your precious freckles,
"Angel kisses," says Aunt Dar.

We send our heartfelt love
On the wings of a snow white dove.

Maybe time will ease our pain,
But our love for you will always remain.

We hold on to the memories of you in our hearts;
There they will stay and never depart.

The angels sing, and the white doves fly,
It's time to say good-bye,
But only for a while.
For when our time here is up, we'll come
join you and again see your Smile.

It hurts so much to let you go,
But now you're pain free—this we know.
With aching hearts, we say good-bye.
We Love you Jess ... God bless
you ... good-bye ... for now!

After Jessie's death, Linda changed. Her laughter is more sporadic, she sleeps a lot and sometimes seems distant and withdrawn. Ever since Jessie's death, Linda ends every visit or phone conversation with, "I love you!" She understands how fleeting life can be. She blamed herself since Jessie was in her care. Her husband was very supportive. Weeks later, he confided in me, "I miss Jessie's giggle the most. The house is so quiet without her." This was extremely painful for me as an uncle; I can't imagine the pain of a parent.

I missed her too. Jessie used to sneak up behind me and tickle the back of my neck. "Hey, what do you think you're doing?" I'd ask. She'd giggle so loudly. Then, she'd sneak back a few minutes later to repeat it. It was a game I loved.

Jessie's death was tragic, but the challenges of life were far from behind us. By August 2007, Becky had become increasingly reclusive. Several times, she'd attempted suicide, but was unsuccessful. After one attempt, she ended up in the hospital. "She needs help!" Mom said to the doctor. "How do we get it for her?"

"We can put her in the stress unit," said the doctor. "But she can walk out after seventy-two hours."

We were frustrated and felt there was little we could do to help.

Beck had such a huge personality. In her teen years and her twenties, she was very fun to be around. She could be the life of the party. When she moved to Hawaii, she and I wrote back and forth frequently. She shared her faith with me. We were both growing in our love for the Lord. This lessened some when the mental illness took over. Her son, Kory, grew up taking care of Becky. In many ways, he was the adult, and Beck the needy child. Kory sacrificed many social activities to stay with Becky. She always wanted him by her side. As time went on, he continued taking care of her as her mental illness worsened. After high school, Kory moved to Wisconsin and got a job not far from where his dad lived. Becky struggled to find peace in her life.

The only peace she found was in death. On August 29, 2007, Becky committed suicide at age fifty-two. Jimmy stopped by and told me the news. "Why did she do this to herself?" I asked. She died from an overdose of prescription meds combined with other drugs. Beck was found by a neighbor, slumped over the arm of her couch. Kory was told by his dad and drove back home. All the terrible pain of losing another family member returned. The only solace was in knowing Becky had truly loved the Lord, and that she was no longer fighting her demons. She was at peace. Much as there was a time when little was known about handicapped individuals, I felt the same about mental illness. I wished I had known more and how to help Becky. Over time, I understood that mental illness is a disease like any other, and it claimed Becky's life.

Though Becky's death was not as sudden and unexpected as Dad and Jessie's, it still came as a shock. And it was incredibly difficult for Kory as they had been very close. But I worried most about Mom. *How much more pain can she go through?* I wondered. In her grief, she said, "You aren't suppose to lose your children and grandchildren before you go!" Somehow, she always remained strong.

The losses our family bore were difficult and painful. We were all so close. We didn't understand why these terrible tragedies happened, but I knew the only way I survived was with my faith. I turned to constant prayer. As a Christian, I believe God has a better place ahead after our earthly journey ends. Someday I'll see my family members again in the glory of heaven. Being a Christian didn't make me immune to pain and heartache, but it allowed me the strength to find my way through these times.

CHAPTER 39
VAN FUNDRAISER

"And as you wish that others would do to you, do so to them."
—Luke 6:31

No one can escape death and loss in life, but what can help alleviate the pain, along with faith and family, is friends. Lyle is a tight-knit community where we care about our neighbors. It's an extended family. When someone is struggling, we reach out to lend a helping hand. In 2006, the year before Becky died, I had a twenty-year-old van that had seen better days. It wasn't reliable anymore, and it wasn't safe to take on long trips because so many functions had been lost. The steering didn't work properly; the gas and oil leaked; I couldn't access the van very easy with my new wheelchair because the lift didn't accommodate properly; and much more. It made no sense to invest money in it.

One afternoon, as I sat outside, my next door neighbor came to visit. I'd known him for years. He was the chief of the Lyle Fire Department, and his wife had graduated with Becky. That day, he told me the fire department had some extra money in a fund, and that they wanted it to go to a local project.

"We've seen you struggling with your van, and we'd like it to go toward an updated van for you," he said.

"I'm not sure about that," I said, overwhelmed by the kind and generous offer.

He was undeterred. "I'm going to talk to a few people, and I'll let you know what I find out," he said.

This was a very kind and generous gesture, but it made me uncomfortable. I wondered if others could benefit from this money more. For some reason, I didn't feel worthy. This project would involve thousands of dollars. I had tried to give all I could to my community, but I never wanted anything in return. Before I knew it, word had spread, and a fundraising committee was formed so I could get an updated van. Once Lyle and surrounding communities see someone in need, there's no stopping them. The fundraiser took on a life of its own. There were articles in the papers and posters up all over.

Since I wasn't comfortable with all of the attention focused on me, I talked to my pastor about my feelings. "Randy," she said, "sometimes you need to let people help you. It makes them feel good to do this." I couldn't argue with her logic and, finally, decided to just let it happen.

The fundraiser was held at Our Savior's Lutheran Church's dining room. There was a big meal for a freewill offering, baked goods for sale, different items given away by people who generously donated them for raffles, sports trivia games, pies and other items to be auctioned off, and more. I was very nervous before the event. What if very few people showed up? Would people want to come? I needn't have worried; God was in charge. The fundraiser turnout was amazing, and I was overwhelmed. There were three hundred or more people who showed up. Not everyone could fit in the dining room at once. People came from all over the area. Some I hadn't seen in years. Others didn't even know me, but read articles and wanted to help. Friends drove from two hours away. That room was filled with so much love that night, and I felt the presence of the Holy Spirit in the kindness and generosity of others.

In the end, enough money was raised for me to get a very nice updated van that is still in great running shape today. It has a lowered floor, allowing me easy access. Push buttons are used to open the side doors, lowering the lift; I wheel on it and am raised to floor level; I wheel in, and sturdy tie downs keep me secure. It has been a Godsend from those who attended the fundraiser that night.

How could I ever thank everyone? I knew that in a small town like Lyle, there are a lot of big hearts. People volunteer to help in any way they can. People don't do it for recognition. They do it because they care about others. They know that without a giving spirit, there's a good chance a small community won't survive. In a way, this fundraiser was the community's way of thanking me for my volunteer efforts: twenty-two years as Lyle's PA announcer and twenty years working in the school. I wanted to thank them back, but I was overcome with emotion. Talk about an act of Christian love put into action that night. It was a night I'll never forget—a night filled with overwhelming giving, love, and compassion. I'm blessed to live in a community where people want to help others.

At home that night, I tilted way back in my wheelchair and looked up at the stars, and then I prayed, "God, thank you for this amazing night. I've been truly blessed with the wonderful people you've surrounded me with. Please let them know how grateful I am."

Giving thanks! (2006)

CHAPTER 40
A BRUSH WITH DEATH

*"Our present sufferings are not worth comparing
to the glory that will be revealed in us."*
—Romans 8:18

In December 2008, I had emergency surgery at St. Marys hospital in Rochester for a bowel obstruction. Jean, my attendant, came to do my cares about 2:00 p.m. I told her my stomach was bothering me and I didn't feel right. Jean emptied my urine bag and did bowel care. I tried drinking water, but couldn't. This is highly unusual, since I normally drink at least twelve glasses a day. Jean noticed my urine bag was still empty. I was having no urine output at all. Again, this is highly unusual. She asked if I wanted her to call 911. After telling her I didn't, I tried drinking cranberry juice. I couldn't, and still no urine output. I was now very concerned. Jean checked for a fever—it was normal. She then noticed my pupils had dilated. I agreed she should call 911. The first responders were there in minutes, followed by the ambulance. They rushed me to the Austin emergency room. By now I was very hot, which is never the case. I'm always on the cold side. Blood tests showed my white blood cell count was dangerously high, and X-rays showed the blockage. Considering my condition, the doctors in Austin figured St. Marys would be the best place for the surgery. I was hurried by ambulance from Austin to Rochester. The surgeon at St. Marys came into the small emergency room and pulled up a chair. I was lying on my side, and Bonnie, Jim's wife, was with me.

"I want to be honest with you," he said. "We need to get you into surgery as soon as possible. We're going in somewhat blind. All we have to go by are the X-rays from Austin. We don't really know what to expect. Hopefully, you won't need to be on a respirator for the rest of your life." This is always a concern since my respiration is very limited. It's a constant worry that I wouldn't breathe on my own once the surgery was over. The surgeon continued, "We might only be able to do part of the surgery today and have to finish it at a later date. You may have a colostomy bag. The best case scenario would be to remove the blockage area and then reconnect your small intestines. Do you have any questions?"

"I don't think so." My head was spinning, but I was already aware of the potential problems that lay ahead because of my paralysis.

"We're going to get a quick X-ray of your lungs, and I'll see you in surgery in a few minutes, okay?" he said before leaving.

I appreciated his honesty. I looked at Bonnie and said, "Sounds pretty serious."

She had tears in her eyes as she said, "Everything will be fine, Ran."

"When you think about it, it's a win-win situation for me," I said, with tears running down my face. "If everything turns out okay, I'll still be able to see my wonderful family and friends. If not, I'll get to go home to the kingdom of heaven."

The staff came to take me for a quick chest X-ray. While waiting for the technician, I prayed, "God, give me the peace and strength to get through this. Look over my family while they wait. Guide the doctors as they perform my surgery. I love You. Amen!" As a soothing balm to my soul, I repeated my favorite Scripture over and over in my head. "I can do all things through Christ who strengthens me." I was rewarded with an overwhelming sense of comfort and peace! I suddenly knew everything would be fine.

After the X-ray, they took me back to my small room in emergency. I saw Mom, and I was blessed with the chance to tell her and my family that I loved them before they whisked me to the operating room. When

I woke in recovery, the nurse said, "Your surgery went fine, and your vitals are looking good. You'll be going to your room in just a few minutes." They had removed three-and-a-half feet of my small intestines and were able to reconnect everything. The best case scenario came to be. I had no after effects. We all wore big smiles on our faces that day.

That experience, like many, reinforced that God was a constant presence in my life. He was there whenever I needed Him. It also gave me a brush with the reality of death. Through it, I learned not to be afraid. And I'm not. God is in control of my timeline. I don't shy away from the possibility of death. It's simply the end result of our earthly lives. My body is a temporary home. When I am finished fulfilling God's plans for me on earth, then I will be called home. We Christians never really say good-bye, because we know about the promise of heaven, where we begin the rest of our lives.

Chapter 41
What a Ride!

"Teaching them to observe all that
I have commanded you.
And behold, I am with you always,
to the end of the age."
—Matthew 28:20

Whether you look at life as a long walk or a wild ride, it is always a journey. My journey may not have been the conventional path many have taken, but it's allowed me to grow into the person I am today.

At the time of my accident, I believed in God and prayed all the time. But as a twelve-year-old kid, my Christian journey had barely begun. I didn't understand the role God would play in my life. I was a confused, frightened, and very scared kid. I was in a dark place filled with uncertainty. There is simply one answer to how I got through living seventeen months in the hospital, away from my family, and paralyzed: God! How else could a scared kid make it through that? God's strength, peace, and grace allowed me the inner faith to get through each day. As my faith grew, my perspective changed. The petty things in life no longer mattered. Instead, I focused on the larger picture. I chose to put God first and lean on Him, and that's what gave me the strength to get through each situation I faced.

The accident and my growing faith also helped me see life with a different set of eyes than before. At a young age, I experienced my first death. I witnessed heartaches, physical and emotional pain, broken families and relationships. I saw compassion, special acts of kindness, and unkind acts. And I experienced joy, jubilation, happiness, and, most important, God's love, strength, and peaceful grace. This completely changed my life. Though my body was made weaker, my spirit was strengthened.

Strength is often associated with physical strength. But I always think of it in terms of what's inside us. Since my body is weak, I became a rock for my family and friends. When they need someone to talk to, I listen. I promise to be there until the end. That's not to say there aren't times when I feel anything but strong. Those are the moments I need to recharge, to turn to God for His unfailing love and strength. I remind myself that He's in control; it gives me the boost I need.

Over time, I've learned not to focus on what I can't do. I can't scratch an itch, swat away a mosquito, get a drink of water, fix my foot if a muscle spasm moves it out of place, pull the sheet back if I'm too hot, feed myself at my preferred pace, talk to someone face-to-face since I sit too low in my chair, feel the weight of an object in my hand, and so much more. Because I need to be turned from one side to the other a couple times during the night, I haven't had a full night's sleep since my accident. There are so many limitations that I can't list them all. The important thing is that these aren't a big deal to me anymore. They are simply part of my life.

Are there other things I miss about my life before the accident? What I miss the most is being able to touch someone. I'd love to reach out and give Mom a hug. What an awesome feeling that would be! Just being able to shake hands with others would be nice. Those who know me well give me a hug when they see me. I sure appreciate that courtesy. While I have limited feeling, I still have feeling. Touch is essential to life, as it promotes wellness and healing.

And I would have loved to experience the privilege and responsibility of being a father and husband. I wondered what it would've been like to hold my wife's hand as she gave birth to our child—part of me. It would've been witnessing a miracle. Playing catch with my kids would've been uplifting. Giving my family time, just as my parents did for me, would've been rewarding. I don't seek sympathy. That's not who I am. I just acknowledge that this is something I missed. It wasn't in God's plan for me, and I've accepted that.

Perhaps the only thing that I haven't been able to get used to is seeing someone take what they have for granted. It makes me angry. When they complain about little chores they have to do or walking a short distance because no one is available to drive them somewhere, I want to holler, "Are you kidding me? Be thankful for all you have because it can be taken from you in a split second." But I don't let anger get the best of me. We all get angry on occasion, because we all struggle. I pray and let go of it quickly, so it doesn't fester inside.

My journey has been different from that of many others, but I'm thankful for it. We can't all walk the same path, but we can be thankful for the blessings along the path we do travel. I've never understood all of the trials I've faced. I don't understand why there is so much pain and suffering in this world. But I always believed my accident happened for a reason. I have confidence that God will one day make it clear to me. While I've waited, I've tried to do whatever I can for others with the gifts I have, despite my limitations. I've enjoyed the ride, and I can't wait until the day I walk side-by-side with Jesus on the shores of heaven!

EPILOGUE

It has been a year and a half since I started writing this book. Another anniversary of my accident has passed—the forty-sixth! I'm proud to have beaten the odds the doctors placed on me. With the extra time God gave me, I feel a sense of responsibility and obligation. I pray I've used the gifts He provided me with to the best of my abilities. It was always important to make my parents proud of me, but it's even more important to make my Heavenly Father proud. I now know God has been in control all along.

God helped me grow into the person I am today. It took me a while, but I can honestly say I like who I am. I still enjoy just living life. I continue living in the same apartment I moved into in 1980.

My family is doing well. Mom is living in the senior citizen housing apartment she moved into in 2006. She is limited in her physical mobility, but with the help of family, friends, and neighbors, she lives a fairly independent lifestyle. Mom will always be the most extraordinary person I've ever met.

Some of my nieces and nephews now have their own families. They are good people with giving spirits. Our family gatherings have grown so much.

Yes, we still have trials and tribulations from time to time, but nothing we can't overcome with family support and God's unending hope, peace, strength, and unconditional love!

I'm still living the guided path God has set forth for me. My unconventional journey continues—and I'd have it no other way!

Giving thanks always and for everything to God the Father in the name of our Lord Jesus Christ.
-Ephesians 5:20